# Cambridge for DGB

**Student's Pack**

**1**

Kenna Bourke

# Acknowledgments

We would like to thank those who contributed to the development of the *Cambridge for DGB* course. Particular thanks are owed to the COBACH teachers and coordinators whose insights and suggestions helped define the content and format of the series, and to the COBACH administrators who graciously facilitated their staff's participation in this project:

**Colegio de Bachilleres del Estado de San Luis Potosí:**
Benjamín Vázquez Gámez
Dagoberto Gerardo Pérez Moreno
Ma. del Pilar Eugenia Alejo Lozada
María Muñoz Guerrero
Misael Mendoza Villeda
Simón Isidro Piña

> Ing. Mónico Jiménez Medina, Director General
> M. Francisco Reyna Turrubiartes, Director Académico
> Miguel Ángel Mendoza Martínez, Jefe de Materia

**Colegio de Bachilleres del Estado de Zacatecas:**
Antonio Díaz Romero
Javier Espinoza Romo
Ricardo Macías Sotelo
Susan García Pérez
Víctor Octavio Espinoza Lozano

> M.C. Felipe Ramírez Chávez, Director General
> Lic. Josefina Martínez Flores, Directora Acádemica
> Lic. Víctor Octavio Espinoza Lozano, Jefe de Materia

**Colegio de Bachilleres del Estado de Querétaro:**
Eva María Alegría Orozco
Alejandro Contreras Clemente

> Maria Teresa Quiroz Bautista, Jefatura del Área de Inglés

**GLACE Language Center, San Luis Potosí**
Karen Marie Golnick
Elvia María Rico Zermeño

**Managing Editor:** Deborah Iddon
**Development Editor:** Kimberly MacCurdy Keithahn

# Introduction

Welcome to **Cambridge for DGB**.

With **Cambridge for DGB** you will learn and use English more effectively.

**Cambridge for DGB** offers you a successful learning experience.
- It segments language learning into manageable pieces of information.
- It provides easy, instant opportunities for oral and written practice.
- It shows you your progress at the end of each lesson.

**Cambridge for DGB** meets the general DGB competences.
- It integrates moments of reflection to develop your intrapersonal skills.
- It fosters pair and group activities to develop your interpersonal skills.
- It includes activities that challenge your thinking and reasoning skills.

**Cambridge for DGB** meets the specific DGB competences. At the end of this level:
- You will be able to understand basic spoken and written communication in English.
- You will be able to express your ideas simply in English.
- You will be able to read this introduction in English.

# Introducción

Bienvenido/a a **Cambridge para DGB**.

Con **Cambridge para DGB** aprenderás y usarás el inglés de manera más efectiva.

**Cambridge para DGB** te ofrece una experiencia de aprendizaje exitosa.
- Divide el aprendizaje de la lengua en partes manejables de información.
- Provee de oportunidades fáciles e instantáneas para la práctica oral y escrita.
- Muestra tu progreso al final de cada lección.

**Cambridge para DGB** cumple con las competencias generales de DGB.
- Integra momentos de reflexión para desarrollar tus habilidades interpersonales.
- Fomenta actividades de pareja y equipos que desarrollan tus habilidades interpersonales.
- Incluye actividades que retan tus habilidades de pensamiento y razonamiento.

**Cambridge para DGB** cubre las competencias específicas de DGB. Al finalizar este nivel:
- Serás capaz de entender comunicaciones escritas y orales básicas.
- Serás capaz de expresar ideas sencillas en inglés.
- Serás capaz de leer esta introducción en inglés.

# Scope and sequence

| LEVEL 1 | LEARNING OUTCOMES | GRAMMAR | VOCABULARY |
|---|---|---|---|
| **Why learn English?** Page 1<br>**Diagnostic tests** Pages 2–5<br>**Classroom language** Pages 6–10 | Students can …<br>- identify reasons for learning English<br>- identify learning opportunities<br>- say hello and goodbye<br>- understand classroom instructions<br>- ask questions<br>- identify classroom objects | | |
| **Unit 1–3**<br>*My world* Pages 11–32 | **Students can …** | | |
| **Unit 1**<br>*It's nice to meet you!* | - introduce themselves<br>- talk about and write personal information | Verb *be*<br>Possessive adjectives<br>Subject pronouns<br>*Yes/No* questions with *be* | Numbers 0–19 |
| **Unit 2**<br>*What are they like?* | - talk and write about family members<br>- describe and write about their family, friends, and themselves | Possessives: *'s* and *s'*<br>Verb *have*<br>Articles: *a*, *an*, and *the* | Family<br>Physical appearance |
| **Unit 3**<br>*Where are you from?* | - ask where people are from and describe their favorite natural places<br>- investigate, write, and talk about indigenous cultures | Question words: *Who?*, *Where?*, *What?*, and *How old?* | Countries, nationalities, geographical features |
| **Unit 4–6**<br>*Lifestyles* Pages 33–54 | **Students can …** | | |
| **Unit 4**<br>*Work and transportation* | - talk about jobs and work activities<br>- ask and answer questions about transportation | Simple present<br>Simple present *yes/no* questions | Jobs<br>Transportation |
| **Unit 5**<br>*Routines and free time* | - describe and write about free-time activities<br>- talk and write about their daily routines | Adverbs of frequency *ever*<br>Simple present *Wh-* questions, *How often?*, and Time expressions | Activities and sports<br>Days of the week and routines |
| **Unit 6**<br>*Community and culture* | - talk about places around town<br>- investigate, write, and talk about indigenous cultures | Prepositions of location | Places around town |

| LANGUAGE IN CONTEXT AND CONVERSATION | LISTENING | READING AND WRITING | SPEAKING AND PRONUNCIATION |
|---|---|---|---|
| | | | ▪ Say hello and goodbye<br>▪ Practice classroom instructions<br>▪ Ask questions<br>▪ Say names of classroom objects |
| **Language in context:**<br>What's your name?<br>**Conversation:**<br>Is your name Ana Garcia? | | | **Speaking:**<br>Meet your classmates<br>– Introductions<br>**Pronunciation:**<br>Phone numbers and email addresses |
| **Language in context:**<br>My sister's name is Elena.<br>**Conversation:**<br>I have a brother and a sister. | | | **Speaking:**<br>My family tree<br>– Information exchange<br>This is me!<br>– Presentation about self or family |
| **Language in context:**<br>What's Peru like? | ▪ Magical Mexico | **Reading:**<br>The Téenek and the Navajo<br>An article<br>**Writing:**<br>My visa application | **Speaking:**<br>My e-pal<br>– Interview and presentation about e-pal<br>My visa interview<br>– Role play of a visa interview |
| **Language in context:**<br>She answers the phone.<br>**Conversation:**<br>Do you take the bus to school? | | | **Speaking:**<br>Transportation interview<br>– Information exchange<br>**Pronunciation:**<br>Third person singular endings |
| **Language in context:**<br>He sometimes listens to music.<br>**Conversation:**<br>What do you do every morning? | | | **Speaking:**<br>My free time<br>– Questions and answers about free time<br>My daily routine<br>– Presentation about daily activities |
| **Language in context:**<br>Leon always goes to the movies on the weekend. | ▪ The famous Triqui basketball players! | **Reading:**<br>The Otomí and the Cora<br>An article<br>**Writing:**<br>Indigenous groups | **Speaking:**<br>E-pal / classmate interview<br>– Interview and presentation about classmates' routines<br>Class presentation<br>– Presentation of indigenous group research |

**Scope and sequence**

| LEVEL 1 | LEARNING OUTCOMES | GRAMMAR | VOCABULARY |
|---|---|---|---|
| **Unit 7–9** *Our activities* Pages 55–76 | **Students can ...** | | |
| **Unit 7** *Our day* | • ask for and tell the time<br>• talk about jobs and work activities | Review of simple present *Wh-* questions<br>Present continuous | Telling the time<br>More jobs |
| **Unit 8** *What's happening?* | • talk about activities people are doing right now<br>• describe online activities and daily routines | Present continuous *yes/no* questions<br>Present continuous with *Wh-* questions | Clothing and colors<br>Online activities |
| **Unit 9** *Our society* | • talk about social issues<br>• write and perform a rap about social issues | Simple present and present continuous | Cyber bullying |
| **Units 10–12** *Let's eat!* Pages 77–98 | **Students can ...** | | |
| **Unit 10** *My town* | • say where places are around town<br>• talk about different foods | *There is / there are;*<br>Prepositions of location<br>Count and noncount nouns | Places around town<br>Food |
| **Unit 11** *Eating out* | • talk about food on a menu<br>• talk about measurements and quantities of food | *Is there...? / Are there...?*<br>*some, any*<br>*How much? / How many?*<br>*a lot of, some, a little,*<br>*a few, much, many, any* | On the menu<br>Measurements and quantities |
| **Unit 12** *My favorite recipes* | • describe different ways to cook food<br>• research recipes and create a cookbook | *How much is / are...?*<br>Numbers 20–101 | Cooking verbs |
| **Level 1** *Our Mexico!* Pages 99–101 | **Students can ...** | | |
| **Level 1 project** | • talk about themselves and their families<br>• talk about communities<br>• describe geographical features<br>• describe traditional Mexican food | All grammar in Level 1 | All vocabulary in Level 1 |
| **Dictionary** Pages 102–107 | | | |
| **Language summaries** Pages 108–115 | | | |
| **Audio scripts** Pages 116–117 | | | |

| LANGUAGE IN CONTEXT AND CONVERSATION | LISTENING | READING AND WRITING | SPEAKING AND PRONUNCIATION |
|---|---|---|---|
| **Language in context:** *What time is it?* <br> **Conversation:** *I'm reading about jobs.* | | | **Pronunciation:** *Reduction of to* <br> **Speaking:** *Act it out!* <br> – Guessing game about actions |
| **Language in context:** *Is Ana watching a movie?* <br> **Conversation:** *What's she doing?* | | | **Speaking:** *Our class closet!* <br> – Survey about favorite clothes <br> *It's Saturday!* <br> – Information exchange about activities |
| **Language in context:** *We don't have time for cyber bullying!* | ▪ *It's early. It's late.* | **Reading:** *Early morning* <br> Song lyrics <br> **Writing:** *Our rap* | **Speaking:** *Breaking news* <br> – Performance about social issues <br> *Rap it!* <br> – Presentation of rap about social issues |
| **Language in context:** *There's a coffee shop.* <br> **Conversation:** *There are strawberries and apples.* | | | **Speaking:** *A town map* <br> – Presentation about a town <br> **Pronunciation:** /s/ and /z/ sounds |
| **Language in context:** *Is there spaghetti today?* <br> **Conversation:** *We need a kilo of chicken.* | | | **Speaking:** *My grocery list* <br> – Presentation about grocery shopping <br> *My favorite food* <br> – Information exchange about favorite food |
| **Language in context:** *How much are strawberries?* | ▪ *Italian food* | **Reading:** *English Sunday Dinner* <br> An article <br> **Writing:** *Our cookbook* | **Speaking:** *Our lunch plans* <br> – Role play of cooking, ordering, or shopping <br> *Class cookbooks* <br> – Presentation about cookbooks |
| | | | **Speaking:** <br> – Survey about people, places, activities, geographical features, and food <br> – Poster presentation about Mexico |

Scope and sequence **vii**

# Walkthrough of the Student's Pack

Every unit of *Cambridge for DGB* contains four pages of activities. Each two-page spread has a personalized speaking or pronunciation activity that provides you with relevant and meaningful practice of the grammar and vocabulary you are learning.

**Opener** The block opener introduces the theme.

## Lifestyles

**UNIT 4 Work and transportation**
- ▶ I can talk about jobs and work activities.
- ▶ I can ask and answer questions about transportation.

**UNIT 5 Routines and free time**
- ▶ I can describe and write about free-time activities.
- ▶ I can talk and write about my daily routine.

**UNIT 6 Community and culture**
- ▶ I can talk about places around town.
- ▶ I can investigate, write, and talk about indigenous cultures.

**Can Do** statements say what *you can do* at the end of each unit.

# Walkthrough of unit content

## The first two units

Each two-page spread of these units contains a complete learning cycle: Vocabulary, Language in context or Conversation, Grammar, and Speaking or Pronunciation. First you learn and practice the language elements and then you use them in a personalized speaking activity.

### Vocabulary
- Learn new vocabulary related to the topic.
- Use pictures, charts, and definitions to understand and practice the words.

### Language in context or Conversation
- Listen to the new words in a conversation.
- See how the language works.
- Preview upcoming grammar.

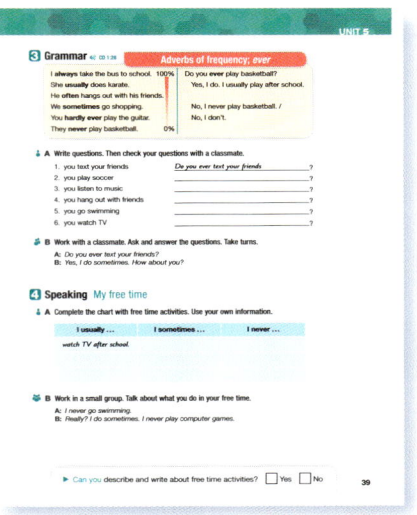

### Grammar
- Listen to and study the examples in the chart.
- Practice the grammar rules in both a written and a short speaking exercise.

### Speaking
- Use the vocabulary and grammar to speak about yourself.
- Answer the **Can Do** questions to confirm your progress.

### Pronunciation
- Identify specific sounds and stress patterns.
- Be able to produce specific sounds and stress patterns.

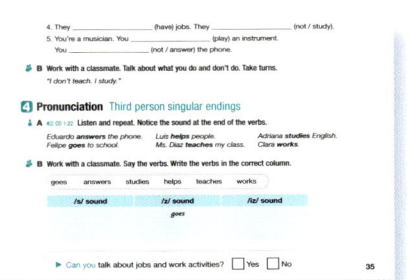

**Walkthrough** ix

# Walkthrough of unit content

## The third unit

The first two pages of the third unit in a block also contain a complete learning cycle: Vocabulary, Language in context, Grammar, and Speaking.

The third and fourth pages of the third unit of each block contain a different learning cycle: Reading, Listening, Writing, and Speaking.

In this learning cycle you practice the **language skills** and then consolidate all your new knowledge in a speaking activity.

### Reading

- Prepare to read by reviewing what you know.
- Read different types of texts.
- Check your comprehension.
- Talk about the reading with your classmates.

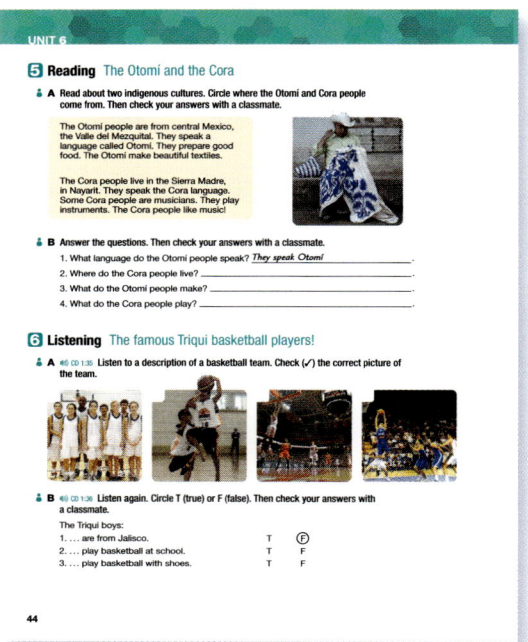

### Listening

- Read the direction line to prepare for the listening task.
- Focus on the important information you hear.
- Listen and check your comprehension.

### Writing

- Work with a classmate or in a small group.
- Investigate a topic.
- Write about a topic.

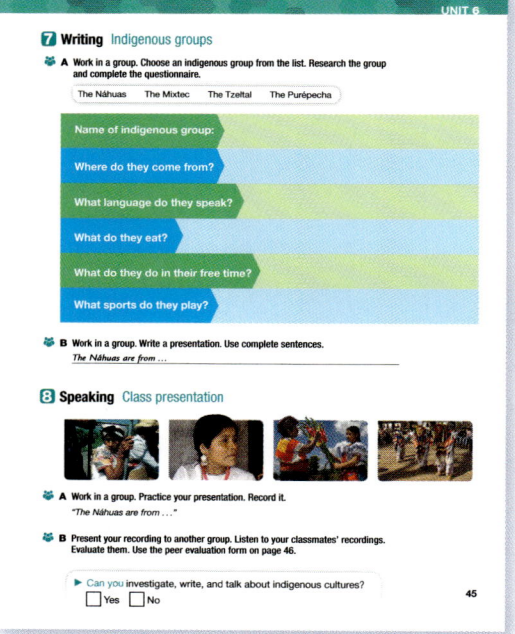

### Speaking

- Work with a classmate or in a group.
- Present your investigation.
- Answer the **Can Do** questions to confirm your progress.

x Walkthrough

# Walkthrough of the Workbook and project

## Workbook

### Practice everything you learn:

- vocabulary
- grammar
- reading

## Level 1 project

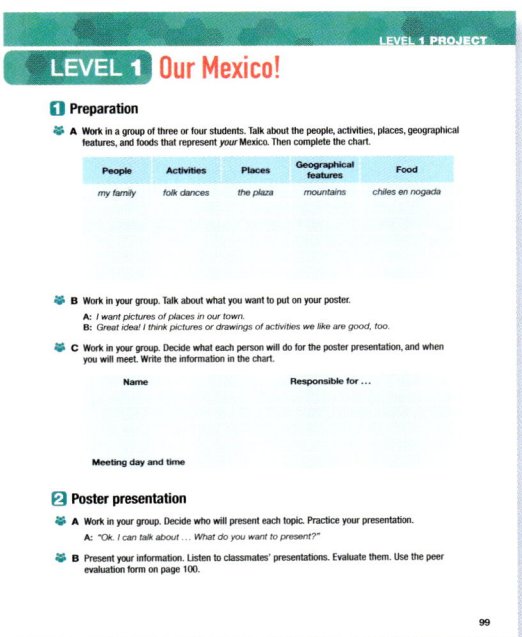

### Work with a group:

- collaborate
- research
- report

Walkthrough   xi

# Walkthrough of evaluation

## Evaluation

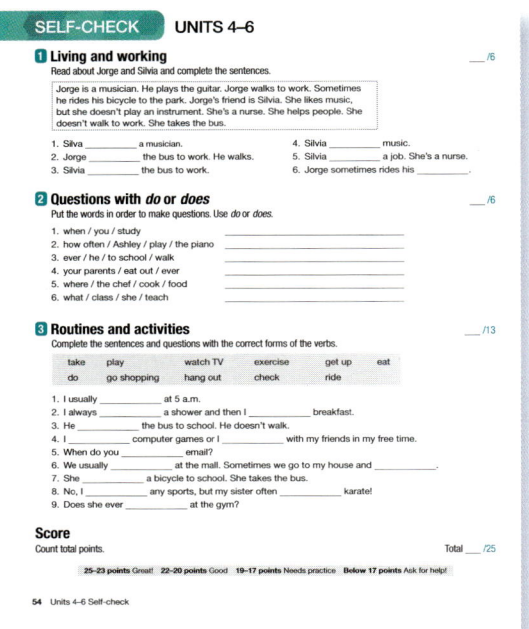

### Self-check

This is an opportunity to check your progress.
Do the exercises. How well can you use the new ...
- grammar?
- vocabulary?

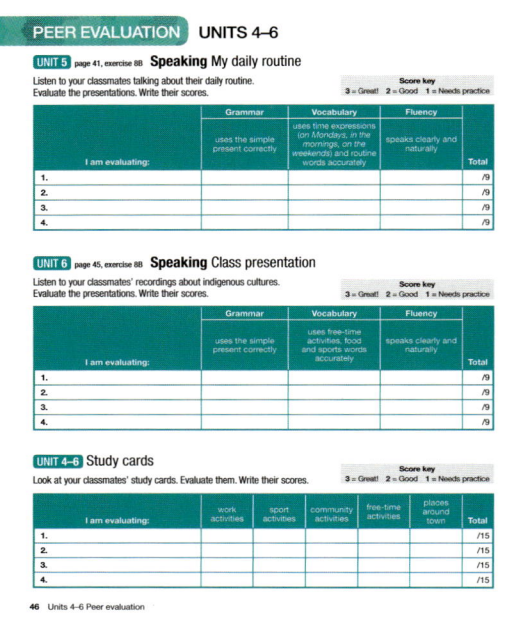

### Peer evaluation

- Evaluate your classmates' work or presentations.
- Use your new language skills to help your classmates improve their language skills.

### Self evaluation

This is an opportunity to think about your progress.
- Read the **Can Do** statements and the examples.
- Can you do these things? Evaluate yourself.

# Why learn English?

## Communication and information

### Internet

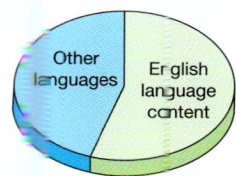

▲ Around 55% of text information on the Internet is in English.

**Learn English:** understand and use information in English from the Internet.

### Networking

▲ More than three billion people use the Internet. Around 30% communicate in English.

**Learn English:** communicate with more people.

## Study and careers

### At school

▲ English is the second language in Mexico's national educational programs.

**Learn English:** do well in school.

### Technical degrees in tourism, manufacturing, and office management

▲ Knowledge of English will give graduates a better chance at finding a job.

**Learn English:** access all the information you will need to help you at work.

## Entertainment

### Music

▲ English is the main language of pop music.

**Learn English:** understand your favorite songs.

### Movies and TV

▲ The top 10 movies of all time are in English.

**Learn English:** watch the movie, not the subtitles.

## Work and travel

### At work

▲ English is the main language of international business, conferences, and advertising.

**Learn English:** open doors to new opportunities.

### Travel

▲ English is the official language in more than 75 countries around the world.

**Learn English:** see the world.

# DIAGNOSTIC TEST — UNITS 1–3

## 1 It's nice to meet you!  ___/10
Circle the correct words.

1. What's **her** / **their** name?
2. **His** / **Her** name **is** / **are** David.
3. **Is** / **Are** you 15 years old?
4. **What's** / **Who's** your phone number?
5. **She's** / **They're** Lucy and Rosa.
6. **They are** / **Are they** students?
7. **I am** / **is** in her class.
8. **Your** / **You're** late today.
9. **A:** Hi. It's nice to meet you.
   **B:** Nice to meet you, too. / Fine, thanks.

## 2 What are they like?  ___/10
Complete the conversation with the words in the box.

**Isa:** Laura _____ two sisters and _____ brother.
**Joe:** _____ her brother like?
**Isa:** He's _____. He has _____ eyes and _____ hair.
**Joe:** _____ her sisters like?
**Isa:** They _____ brown eyes.
**Joe:** _____ his cousin?
**Isa:** His _____ name is Luis.

| a | tall |
| --- | --- |
| What are | cousin's |
| have | green |
| What's | curly |
| has | Who's |

## 3 Where are you from?  ___/5
Circle the correct option.

1. He's Spanish. He's from _____ .
   a. Mexico   b. Spain   c. Chile   d. Peru

2. She's from Great Britain. She's _____ .
   a. Britain   b. Ireland   c. United Kingdom   d. British

3. _____ is Italian?
   a. How old   b. Who   c. What's   d. Where's

4. _____ is she from?
   a. Where   b. What   c. Who   d. How old

5. It's _____ .
   a. a lake   b. a waterfall   c. a beach   d. a desert

Total points: ___/25

# DIAGNOSTIC TEST — UNITS 4–6

## 1 Work and transportation ___/8
Choose the correct answers.

1. Madison and Ashley _____ food.
   a. cooks          b. cook

2. She _____ people. She's a nurse.
   a. studies        b. helps

3. _____ your sisters play the piano?
   a. Do             b. Does

4. He _____ a job.
   a. have           b. has

5. I _____ a car to school. I walk.
   a. don't drive    b. drive

6. _____ a waiter bring food?
   a. Does           b. Do

7. They _____ the bus to school.
   a. take           b. drive

8. My parents work. They _____ to school.
   a. don't go       b. doesn't go

## 2 Routines and free time ___/9
Match the questions and answers.

1. What do you in your free time? ___
2. Do your friends ever listen to music? ___
3. Who do you hang out with? ___
4. Does your mom ever go shopping? ___
5. Where do you and your friends hang out? ___
6. How do you get to school? ___
7. Does your dad ever drive to work? ___
8. When do you watch TV? ___
9. What do you eat for lunch? ___

a. I take the bus.
b. Yes, she does.
c. On the weekends.
d. Yes, they do.
e. My friends.
f. A sandwich.
g. At the park.
h. I play computer games.
i. Yes, he does.

## 3 Community and culture ___/8
Write the correct words.

gym   movies   to   restaurants   to   park   at   café

1. Do you ever go _____ the mall?
2. We like eating out in _____.
3. I go _____ the park every afternoon.
4. Maria checks her email _____ the internet café.
5. My dad exercises in a _____.
6. What's on at the _____ this week?
7. Let's have a latte at the _____.
8. We often play soccer in the _____.

Total points: ___/25

# DIAGNOSTIC TEST   UNITS 7–9

## 1 Our day                                                                   ___/8
Match the questions to the answers.

1. What does Vero do on Sundays? ___
2. When do you see your friends? ___
3. What time do you get up? ___
4. Who do you see on the weekends? ___
5. What's the time? ___
6. What does an accountant do? ___
7. Who responds to emergencies? ___
8. What job do you want to do? ___

a. My grandparents.
b. I want to be a pilot.
c. She plays soccer.
d. He works with numbers.
e. On the weekends.
f. It's a quarter after three.
g. Police officers.
h. At seven o'clock in the morning.

## 2 What's happening?                                                         ___/8
Circle the correct words to complete the sentences.

1. Right now I **watch** / **am watching** a movie.
2. You **aren't** / **don't** studying.
3. She's surfing the **email** / **Internet**.
4. Luis **playing** / **is playing** tennis.
5. Sarah and Daniel **aren't** / **isn't** eating dinner.
6. They are **listening** / **downloading** to music.
7. In the summer, I don't wear a **sweater** / **shirt**.
8. Maru isn't **sing** / **singing** a song.

## 3 Our society                                                               ___/9
Complete the sentences with the words below.

| do   don't   doing   watches   listening   watching   hang out   eat   eating |

1. **A:** What are you doing, Lety?
   **B:** I'm _____ my homework. What about you?
   **A:** I _____ my homework in the evenings. Right now I'm _____ to music.

2. **A:** Do you exercise on the weekends, William?
   **B:** No, I _____ exercise on the weekends. I _____ with my friends.

3. **A:** Hi, Joe. Are you _____ dinner?
   **B:** Yes! We always _____ dinner at eight.

4. **A:** My sister _____ movies every weekend. Does your brother like movies?
   **B:** Yes! He's _____ a movie right now!

Total points: ___/25

# DIAGNOSTIC TEST — UNITS 10–12

## 1 My town  ___/9
Circle the correct words.

1. There **is** / **are** three potatoes **on** / **at** the table.
2. The supermarket is **on** / **between** the bank and the bookstore.
3. There **are** / **is** yogurt **in** / **at** the refrigerator.
4. There is a gas station **next to** / **between** the supermarket.
5. There **aren't** / **isn't** any banks in town.
6. There **is** / **are** books **on** / **in** the bookstore.

## 2 Eating out  ___/9
Circle the correct words to complete the sentences.

1. How _____ cheese is there?
   a. many         b. much

2. There isn't _____ pizza!
   a. any          b. some

3. _____ there any milk?
   a. Are          b. Is

4. How _____ carrots are there?
   a. much         b. many

5. We need _____ rice.
   a. a lot of     b. many

6. There _____ any strawberries.
   a. aren't       b. isn't

7. _____ any sugar?
   a. Is there     b. Are there

8. A _____ of chicken costs $100 pesos.
   a. stick        b. kilo

9. Apples are a _____.
   a. fruit        b. vegetable

## 3 My favorite recipes  ___/7
Complete the sentences with the words below. Choose the best answer.

mix   measure   chop   boil   melt   bake   roast

1. _____ the flour and sugar together.
2. _____ the butter.
3. _____ the vegetables.
4. _____ the water.
5. _____ a cake.
6. _____ a chicken.
7. _____ 500 grams of flour.

Total points: ___/25

# Classroom language

## Saying hello

**A:** *Hey. How's it going?*
**B:** *Hi. Fine, thanks.*

**A:** *Hi. How are you doing?*
**B:** *Hello. I'm OK, thanks. How are you?*

*Good morning. (Hello)*

*Good afternoon. (Hello)*

*Good evening. (Hello or goodbye)*

👥 **Say hello to a classmate.**

# Classroom language

## Saying goodbye

A: See you later, Carolina.
B: Bye, Diego.

A: Goodbye, Andrea.
B: Bye. See you tomorrow.

A: See you later.
B: See you.

👥 Greet a classmate and then say goodbye.

# Classroom language

## Teacher's instructions

Go to page ___.

Listen and repeat.

Read.

Write.

Underline.

Circle.

Work by yourself.

Work with a classmate.

Work in a group.

Check your answers with a classmate.

Ask and answer questions.

Take turns.

 Work with a classmate. Say one of the teacher's instructions. Your partner mimes the action. Take turns.

# Classroom language

## Useful questions

How do you say pizarrón?
Whiteboard.
Not *How you say …?*

What does listen mean?
Escuchar.
Not *What means …?*

How do you spell eraser?
e-r-a-s-e-r
Not *How do you write …?*

Can I go to the restroom, please?

Can I borrow a pen, please?
Sure. Here.

👥 Work with a classmate. Ask and answer the questions. Take turns.

# Classroom language

## Classroom objects

pencil

pen

eraser

notebook

textbook

chair

desk

whiteboard

👥 **Work with a classmate. Ask and answer the questions. Use classroom objects. Take turns.**

1. How do you say _____?
2. How do you spell _____?
3. What does _____ mean?
4. Can I borrow a _____?

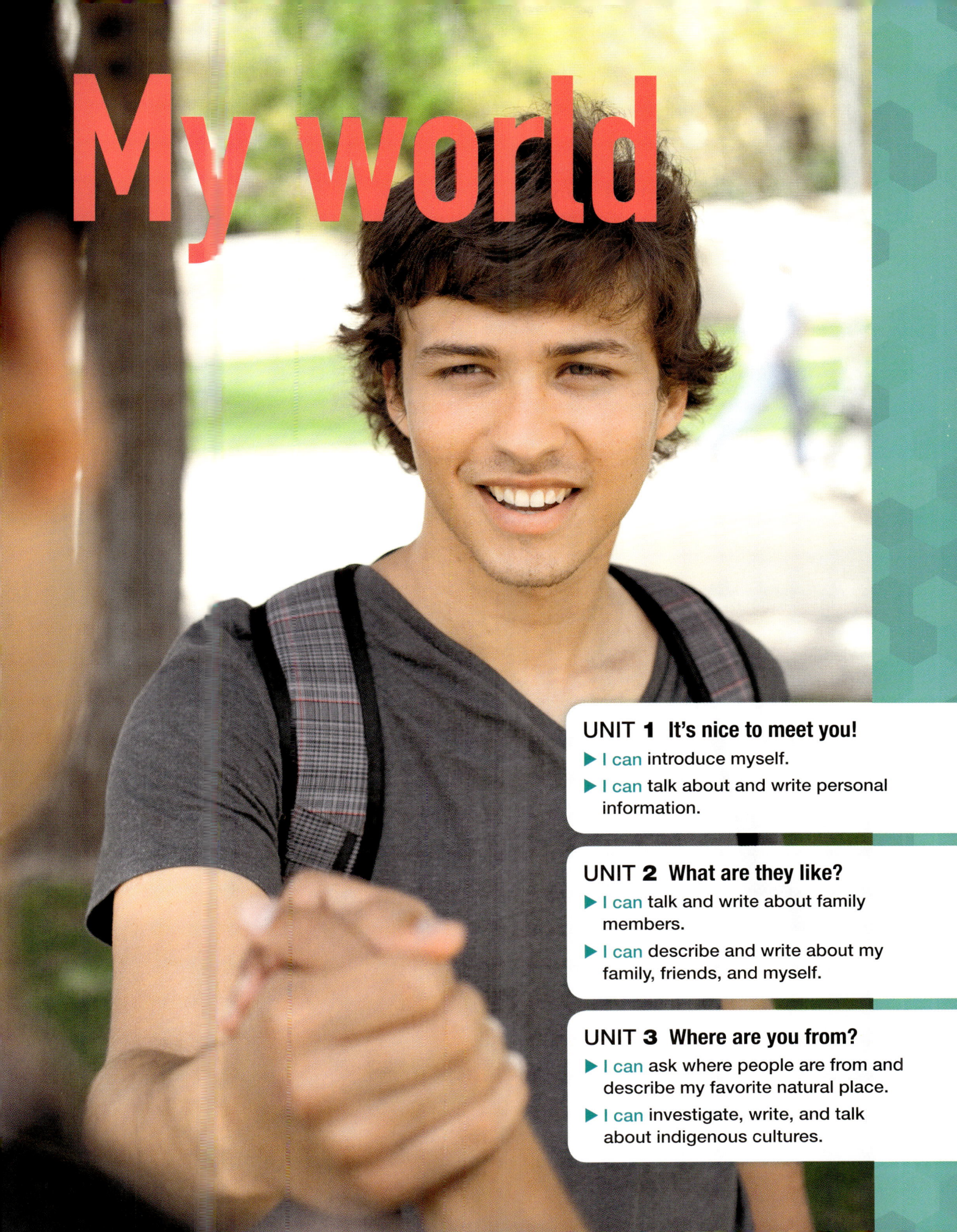

# My world

**UNIT 1  It's nice to meet you!**
▶ I can introduce myself.
▶ I can talk about and write personal information.

**UNIT 2  What are they like?**
▶ I can talk and write about family members.
▶ I can describe and write about my family, friends, and myself.

**UNIT 3  Where are you from?**
▶ I can ask where people are from and describe my favorite natural place.
▶ I can investigate, write, and talk about indigenous cultures.

# UNIT 1  It's nice to meet you!

## 1 Language in context  *What's your name?*

**A**  CD 1:02  Listen. <u>Underline</u> the names.

Hello! My name is <u>Arturo Garcia</u>. What's your name?

Hi, Arturo. My name is Avery Walker. Nice to meet you!

What are their names?

His name is David. Her name's Megan.

Hi! My name's Josh. What are your names?

Hi, Josh! My name is Silvia. Their names are Melissa and Sofia.

**B**  Work with a classmate. Check your answers.

UNIT 1

## 2 Grammar 🔊 CD 1:03

**Verb *be*; possessive adjectives**

| What is (What's) | your name? | My name's Emily. |
| | his name? | His name is Carlos. |
| | her name? | Her name is Marcela. |
| What are | your names? | Our names are Diego and Nancy. |
| | their names? | Their names are Ivan and Gabriela. |

What's = What is
name's = name is
**Your** is singular **and** plural.

**A** Circle the correct words.

1. My name's Teresa. What's **my / (your)** name?
2. She's in our class. **His / Her** name is Leticia.
3. **His / Her** name is Martin Ramos.
4. **Her / Their** names **is / are** Abby and Daniel.
5. Our names **is / are** Alicia and Victor.
6. My name **is / are** Matt. What are **his / your** names?

**B** Work with a classmate. Check your answers.

## 3 Speaking   Meet your classmates

**A** Read the conversation.

Eduardo: Hi! My name is Eduardo Diaz. What's your name?
Alison: Hi, Eduardo! My name is Alison Brown.
Eduardo: It's nice to meet you!
Alison: Nice to meet you, too.

Eduardo: What's his name?
Alison: His name's Tom. What are their names?
Eduardo: Their names are Lisa and Ivan.

**B** Work with a classmate. Introduce yourself. Ask about other classmates.

"Hi! My name is …"

▶ Can you introduce yourself?   ☐ Yes   ☐ No

13

# UNIT 1

## 4 Vocabulary Numbers 0–19

**A** 🔊 CD 1:04 **Listen and repeat.**

| 0 (zero) | 1 (one) | 2 (two) | 3 (three) | 4 (four) | 5 (five) | 6 (six) | 7 (seven) | 8 (eight) | 9 (nine) |
|---|---|---|---|---|---|---|---|---|---|
| 10 (ten) | 11 (eleven) | 12 (twelve) | 13 (thirteen) | 14 (fourteen) | 15 (fifteen) | 16 (sixteen) | 17 (seventeen) | 18 (eighteen) | 19 (nineteen) |

**B** Work with a classmate. Say a number. Your partner writes the word. Check your answers. Take turns.

1. _____
2. _____
3. _____
4. _____
5. _____
6. _____

## 5 Conversation *Is your name Ana Garcia?*

**A** 🔊 CD 1:05 **Listen.**

**Visa official:** Is your name Ana Garcia?
**Ana:** Yes, it is.
**Visa official:** Ok. Thank you. Are you 16 years old?
**Ana:** Yes, I am.
**Visa official:** Ok. Is your phone number 910-555-8364?
**Ana:** No, it's not. It's 910-555-8374.
**Visa official:** Great, thanks. Is your email ana.garcia15@cup.org?
**Ana:** Yes, it is.

**B** Practice the conversation with a classmate. Take turns.

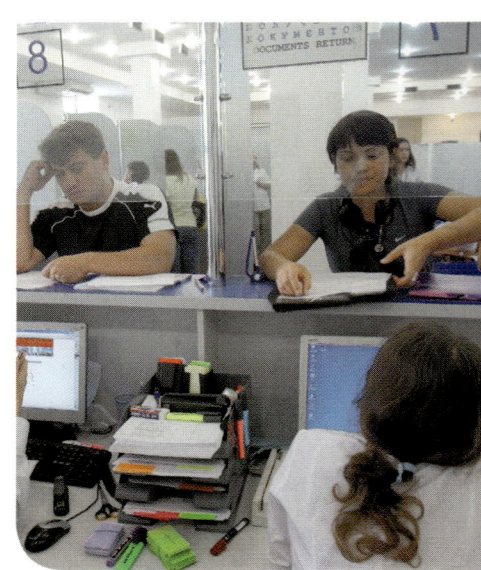

14

## 6 Grammar 🔊 CD 1:06 — Subject pronouns; yes/no questions with be

| | | |
|---|---|---|
| **Am I** in your class? | Yes, **you are**. | No, **you're** not. |
| **Are you** sixteen years old? | Yes, **I am**. | No, **I'm** not. |
| **Is he** your teacher? | Yes, **he is**. | No, **he's** not. |
| **Is she** here today? | Yes, **she is**. | No, **she's** not. |
| **Is your** last name Gomez? | Yes, **it is**. | No, **it's** not. |
| **Are you** Sonia and Jane? | Yes, **we are**. | No, **we're** not. |
| **Are they** in our class? | Yes, **they are**. | No, **they're** not. |

💡 I'm = I am   you're = you are   he's = he is   she's = she is
it's = it is   we're = we are   they're = they are

**A** Match the questions to the correct answers.

1. Is Carmen a student? __c__
2. Are we late? ____
3. Are you 17 years old? ____
4. Is your last name Ortiz? ____
5. Is he in the right class? ____
6. Are they teachers? ____

a. No, they're not. They're students.
b. Yes, he is.
c. Yes, she is. She's in my class.
d. No, we're not.
e. Yes, it is.
f. No, I'm not. I'm 16.

**B** Work with a classmate. Check your answers.

## 7 Pronunciation  Phone numbers and email addresses

**A** 🔊 CD 1:07  Listen and repeat.

910-555-8364 = "nine-one-oh **(zero)**, five-five-five, eight-three-six-four"
ana.gomez15@cup.org = "ana-**dot**-gomez-one-five-**at**-c-u-p-**dot**-org"

"My phone number is 910-555-2736.
My email address is mbrown2@cup.org."

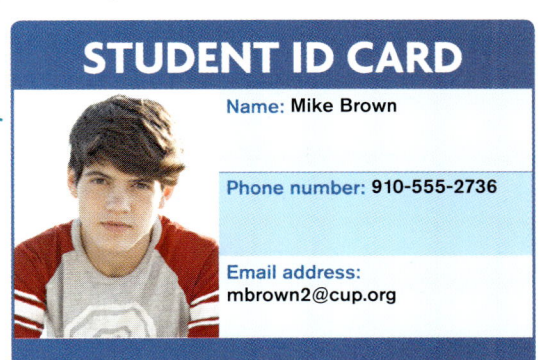

**STUDENT ID CARD**
Name: Mike Brown
Phone number: 910-555-2736
Email address: mbrown2@cup.org

**B** Work with a classmate. Say your phone number and email address. Your partner writes them. Check your answers. Take turns.

Phone number: _____
Email address: _____

▶ Can you talk about and write personal information?   ☐ Yes   ☐ No

# UNIT 2  What are they like?

## 1  Vocabulary  Family

**A** Complete Javier's family tree. Use the words below.

~~grandmother~~   aunt   ~~father/dad~~   sister   ~~cousin~~   grandfather   mother/mom   uncle   brother

Sergio and Martha are Javier's *parents*.
Daniel and Javier are their *sons*.
Ana is their *daughter*.
Daniel, Javier, and Ana are their *children*.

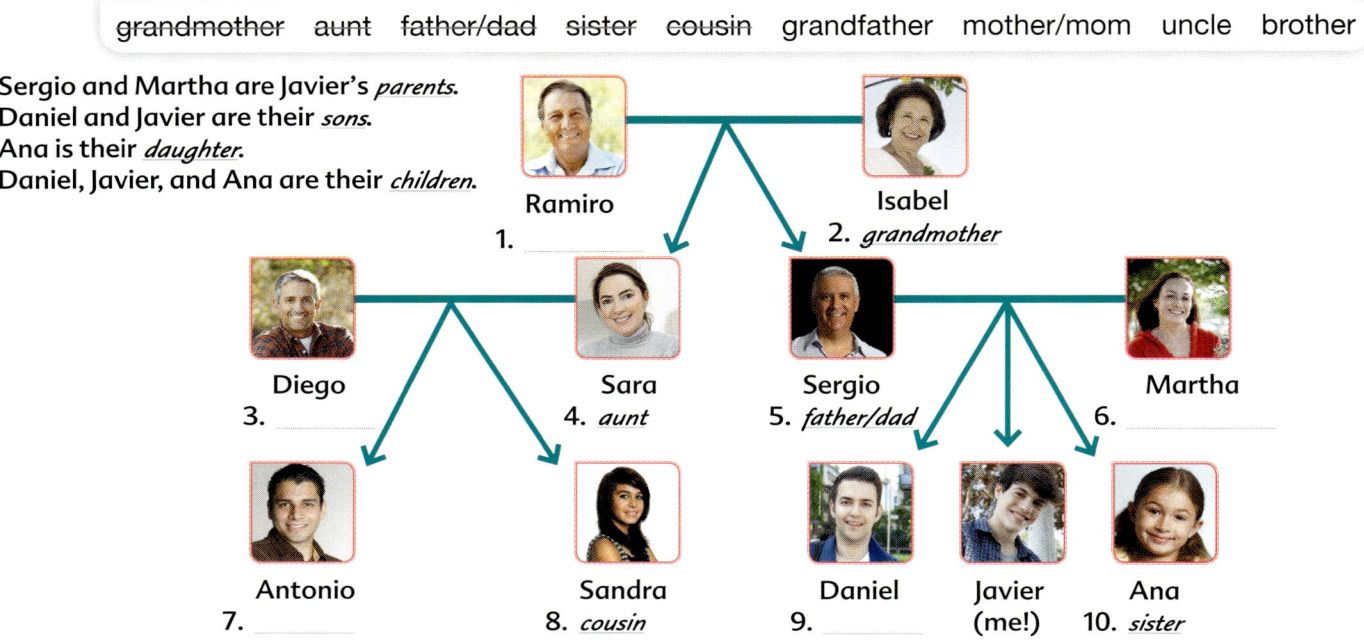

1. _____
2. *grandmother*
3. _____
4. *aunt*
5. *father/dad*
6. _____
7. _____
8. *cousin*
9. _____
10. *sister*

**B**  CD 1:08  Work with a classmate. Listen and check your answers.

## 2  Language in context  *My sister's name is Elena.*

**A**  CD 1:09  Listen to Lucia and Enrique talk about their families. Circle the family vocabulary. Then check your answers with a classmate.

My name is Lucia. My (sister's) name is Elena. My brother's name is Martin. My cousins' names are Gloria and Antonio.

My name is Enrique. My parents' names are Paola and Juan. My aunt's name is Alicia. My uncle's name is Enrique, too.

**B** Work with a classmate. Say the names of three family members. Take turns.

"My mom's name is Malena. My brother's name is …"

16

## 3 Grammar 🔊 CD 1:10

**Possessives: 's and s'**

| Who is **Javier's** sister? | Ana is **Javier's** sister. |
| Who are **Javier's** cousins? | Antonio and Sandra are **Javier's** cousins. |
| What's his **sister's** name? | His **sister's** name is Ana. |
| What are his **cousins'** names? | His **cousins'** names are Antonio and Sandra. |

💡 's = singular
s' = plural

**A** Look at Javier's family tree on page 16. Answer the questions.

1. Find Javier. Who's Javier's brother?  *Daniel is Javier's brother.*
2. Find Sandra. Who's Sandra's dad?  _____
3. Find Antonio. What's his uncle's name?  _____
4. Find Ana. Who's Ana's mom?  _____
5. Find Sergio. What are his parents' names?  _____
6. Find Sandra. Who are Sandra's cousins?  _____

**B** Work with a classmate. Check your answers.

## 4 Speaking  My family tree

**A** Draw your family tree. Use family vocabulary.

**B** Work with a classmate. Ask and answer questions about your family. Take turns.

**A:** What's your sister's name?
**B:** My sister's name is …

▶ Can you talk and write about family members?  ☐ Yes  ☐ No

UNIT 2

## 5 Vocabulary Physical appearance

CD 1:11 Listen and repeat.

### Eyes

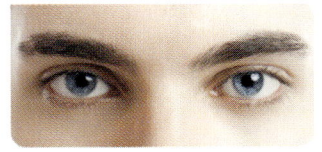 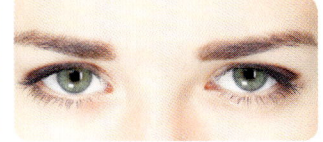 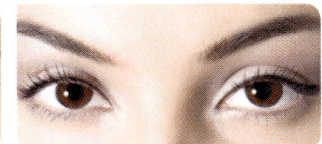

blue eyes    green eyes    brown eyes

### Hair

blond hair    brown hair    red hair    black hair    gray hair

 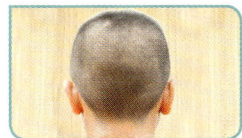   

long hair    short hair    curly hair    straight hair    bald

### Height and build

short  average height  tall       thin    overweight

## 6 Conversation *I have a brother and a sister.*

**A** CD 1:12 Listen.

**Alma:** *I have a brother and a sister.*
**Juan:** *What's your brother like?*
**Alma:** *He is tall and thin. He has curly red hair.*
**Juan:** *What's your sister like?*
**Alma:** *She is average height. She has green eyes.*
**Juan:** *What are your cousins like?*
**Alma:** *They are short. They have straight brown hair and brown eyes.*

**B** Practice the conversation with a classmate. Take turns.

## 7 Grammar 🔊 CD 1:13

**Verb *have*; articles *a*, *an*, and *the***

| I | | | |
|---|---|---|---|
| You | | a sister. | |
| We | have | an aunt. | a + consonant sound |
| They | | a cousin. | an + vowel sound |
| | | | |
| He | | an uncle. | |
| She | has | a brother. | |

I have two aunts. One has brown eyes, and one has green eyes. → **The** aunt with green eyes lives in Mexico City.

💡 *a* and *an* are singular

**A** Complete the sentences. Use *has/have*, *a/an*, or *the*. Then check your answers with a classmate.

1. Joe __has__ three brothers and __a__ sister.
2. We _____ two cousins. They're tall. They _____ green eyes.
3. Eva _____ two uncles and _____ aunt. They _____ curly brown hair.
4. He _____ two sisters. One _____ brown hair. One has blond hair. _____ sister with blond hair is tall.
5. They _____ _____ sister and _____ brother. Their brother _____ blond hair.
6. Raul _____ _____ uncle, _____ aunt, and five cousins. His uncle _____ blue eyes.

**B** Work with a classmate. Describe your best friend. Take turns.

"My best friend is Roberto. He has brown hair. He has a brother and two sisters."

## 8 Speaking  This is me!

**A** Write a description of yourself or a family member.

**B** Work in a small group. Present your description. Listen to your classmates' descriptions. Ask and answer questions. Evaluate the presentations. Use the peer evaluation form on page 24.

**A:** What are your sisters' names?
**B:** Their names are Cristina and Melissa.

*I am average height.*
*I have two sisters.*
*I have long hair. I have…*

▶ Can you write about and describe yourself, your family, and your friends?   ☐ Yes   ☐ No

# UNIT 3 Where are you from?

## 1 Vocabulary  Countries, nationalities, and geographical features

**A** 🔊 CD 1:14  Countries and nationalities. Listen and repeat.

| | Country | Nationality | | Country | Nationality |
|---|---|---|---|---|---|
| 🇦🇺 | Australia | Australian | 🇬🇧 | Great Britain | British |
| 🇧🇷 | Brazil | Brazilian | 🇮🇹 | Italy | Italian |
| 🇨🇦 | Canada | Canadian | 🇲🇽 | Mexico | Mexican |
| 🇨🇱 | Chile | Chilean | 🇵🇪 | Peru | Peruvian |
| 🇨🇳 | China | Chinese | 🇪🇸 | Spain | Spanish |

**B** 🔊 CD 1:15  Geographical features. Write the words under the pictures. Then listen and check your answers.

> waterfall    desert    ocean    beach    mountain    rainforest

1. _beach_   2. _____   3. _____   4. _rainforest_   5. _____   6. _____

## 2 Language in context  *What's Peru like?*

**A** 🔊 CD 1:16  Listen to Lily and Lucas talk about their countries. Circle the geographical features. Then check your answers with a classmate.

Hi! I'm Lily. I'm from Peru. What's Peru like? It's a beautiful country. It's on the Pacific (Ocean). It has beaches, mountains, and waterfalls. This is a waterfall in Peru – the Gocta Falls.

Hello – my name's Lucas. I'm Brazilian. What's Brazil like? It's a big country on the Atlantic (Ocean). It has beaches and rainforests. This is the Amazon rainforest.

**B** Work with a classmate. Describe your favorite natural place in Mexico. What's it like?

*"My favorite natural place is …"*

# UNIT 3

## 3 Grammar 🔊 CD 1:17

**Question words: *Who?*, *Where?*, *What?*, and *How old?***

| | |
|---|---|
| **Who** is Brazilian? | Lucas is Brazilian. |
| **How old** are you? | I'm 16. |
| **Where** are you from? | I'm from Peru. |
| **What's** Peru like? | It's beautiful. |

💡 Use **be** for ages, not **have**: I **am** 16. (Not: I ~~have~~ 16.)

**A** Complete the questions with *Who, Where, What,* or *How old?* Then check your answers with a classmate.

1. __What__ is your name?
2. _____ are you?
3. _____ is your phone number?
4. _____ is your best friend?
5. _____ are you from?
6. _____ is Mexico like?

**B** Work with a classmate. Ask and answer the questions. Take turns.

## 4 Speaking  My e-pal

**A** Interview a student from another high school online. Ask about their appearance, their family, and where they live. Write the information below.

**A:** Where is your family from?
**B:** We are from Chihuahua.

_His family is from Chihuahua._ _____

**B** Work in a small group. Present your information. Take turns.

> My e-pal is Alex Morales. He's 16 years old. He is tall.
> He has brown eyes and brown hair. His family is from Chihuahua...
> _____
> _____
> _____
> _____
> _____
> _____
> _____

▶ Can you ask where people are from and describe your favorite natural place?  ☐ Yes  ☐ No

21

UNIT 3

## 5 Reading  The Téenek and the Navajo

**A** Work in a group. What are some indigenous cultures? Write their names.

Huichol          Apache          _____          _____

**B** Read about the Téenek and the Navajo.

The Téenek are an indigenous group from San Luis Potosí, Hidalgo, Veracruz, and Tamaulipas. They are average height. Many of the Téenek have brown eyes and straight brown hair. They are famous for their traditional embroidery called *quexquémitl*.

The Navajo are a Native American group from Arizona, New Mexico, and Utah. The area they live in is called the Navajo Nation, and they have an independent government. They are average height, and many of the Navajo have brown eyes and straight brown hair, too. They are famous for their turquoise jewelry.

**C** Answer the questions. Then check your answers with a classmate.

1. Where are the Téenek and the Navajo from?
   *The Téenek are from San Luis Potosí, Hidalgo, Veracruz, and Tamaulipas. The Navajo are from…*
   _____

2. What are they like?
   _____

3. What are they famous for?
   _____

## 6 Listening  Magical Mexico

**A**  CD 1:18  Listen to descriptions of places in Mexico. Number the photos from 1 to 4.

**B** Work with a classmate. Check your answers.

UNIT 3

## 7 Writing  My visa application

**A** Complete the visa application.

**VISA APPLICATION**

First name: _____    Last name: _____

Age: _____    Nationality: _____

Eye color: _____    Hair color: _____

**B** Work with a classmate. Look at his or her application. Check the information.

## 8 Speaking  My visa interview

**A** Work with a classmate. Student A is a visa official. Student B is applying for a visa. Write the conversation here. Look at page 14, exercise 5A for ideas.

*Hello. What's your name?* _____

_____

_____

_____

_____

_____

_____

**B** Work in a small group. Present your role play to your classmates. Take turns.

**A:** *Hello. What's your name?*
**B:** *Hi! My name's ...*

▶ Can you investigate, write, and talk about indigenous cultures?  ☐ Yes  ☐ No

23

# PEER EVALUATION UNIT 2

**UNIT 2** page 19, exercise 8B  **Speaking** This is me!

Listen to your classmates talking about themselves and their family. Evaluate the presentations.

**Score key**
3 = Great!   2 = Good   1 = Needs practice

| I am evaluating: | Grammar — uses the verbs *have* and *be* correctly | Vocabulary — uses physical appearance and family words accurately | Fluency — speaks clearly and naturally | Total |
|---|---|---|---|---|
| 1. | | | | /9 |
| 2. | | | | /9 |
| 3. | | | | /9 |
| 4. | | | | /9 |
| 5. | | | | /9 |
| 6. | | | | /9 |
| 7. | | | | /9 |
| 8. | | | | /9 |

# SELF EVALUATION — UNITS 1–3

Read the sentences. Write your score for each.

**Score key**
3 = I can do this very well   2 = I can do this   1 = I need more practice

| What I can do | Score |
|---|---|
| 1. I can introduce myself.<br>Hi. My name is Nancy. |  |
| 2. I can talk about and write personal information.<br>My phone number is 910-555-7234.<br>What's your email address? |  |
| 3. I can talk and write about family members.<br>My mother's name is Genoveva. My father's name is Pedro.<br>My sister's name is Julia. |  |
| 4. I can describe and write about my family, friends, and myself.<br>I'm average height. I have brown hair. My sisters have green eyes.<br>My father is tall. My mother is short. |  |
| 5. I can ask where people are from and describe my favorite natural place.<br>Where are you from?<br>I'm from Querétaro. My favorite place is the beach. It's beautiful. |  |
| 6. I can investigate, write, and talk about indigenous cultures.<br>The Téenek are from San Luis Potosí.<br>They are famous for their traditional embroidery. |  |
| Total |  |

# UNIT 1  It's nice to meet you!

**1 Complete the conversation.**

**Ivan:** Hi. My name __is__ Ivan. What _____ your names?
                    1                              2

**David:** Hi, Ivan. _____ name is David.
                        3

**Lily:** Hello. My name is Lily. _____ name _____ Lauren.
                                      4                5

**Ivan:** It's nice to meet you.

**Lily:** Nice to meet you, too.

**Sofia:** What are __their__ names?
                         6

**Pedro:** _____ name is Jason. Her name _____ Sarah.
              7                                    8

**Sofia:** What _____ _____ last names?
                    9            10

**Pedro:** Sorry. I don't know.

**2 Match the two parts to make sentences.**

1. His name __c__
2. What's ____
3. Their names ____
4. What are ____
5. What ____
6. My ____

a. are Carmen and John.
b. are your names?
c. is David.
d. name is Leticia.
e. her name?
f. their names?

**3 Complete the crossword. Spell the numbers.**

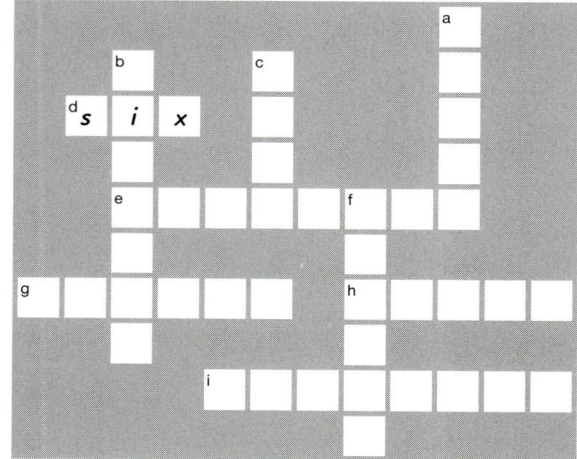

Across →
d. 6
e. 13
g. 12
h. 8
i. 19

Down ↓
a. 7
b. 15
c. 4
f. 11

## 4  Check (✓) the correct responses.

1. Are you in my English class?
   - [✓] Yes, I am
   - [ ] Yes, you are.
2. Is he here?
   - [ ] No, he aren't.
   - [ ] No, he isn't.
3. Are you and David fifteen years old?
   - [ ] No, we aren't.
   - [ ] No, they aren't.
4. Am I on the list?
   - [ ] Yes, I am.
   - [ ] Yes, you are.
5. Are they here today?
   - [ ] Yes, they is.
   - [ ] Yes, they are.
6. Is your last name Diaz?
   - [ ] No, it isn't.
   - [ ] No, it aren't.

## 5  Put the words in the correct order to make questions.

**EXCHANGE STUDENT APPLICATION**

Name: Javier Ortiz          Phone number: 915-555-0173

Age: 16                     Email: javier.ortiz32@cup.org

1. his / number / Is / 912-555-0162 / phone
   Is his phone number 912-555-0162 ?

2. name / his / last / What's
   _____ ?

3. 18 / Is / years / he / old
   _____ ?

4. email / his / javier.ortiz32@cup.org / Is
   _____ ?

## 6  Look at the exchange student application information. Answer the questions in exercise 5. Use complete sentences

1. No, it isn't. It's 915-555-0173 .
2. _____ .
3. _____ .
4. _____ .

# UNIT 2  What are they like?

**1** Look at Isabel's family tree. Write the family words under the pictures.

| sister | father / dad | brother | ~~grandfather~~ | mother / mom |
|---|---|---|---|---|
| cousin | aunt | uncle | grandmother | cousin |

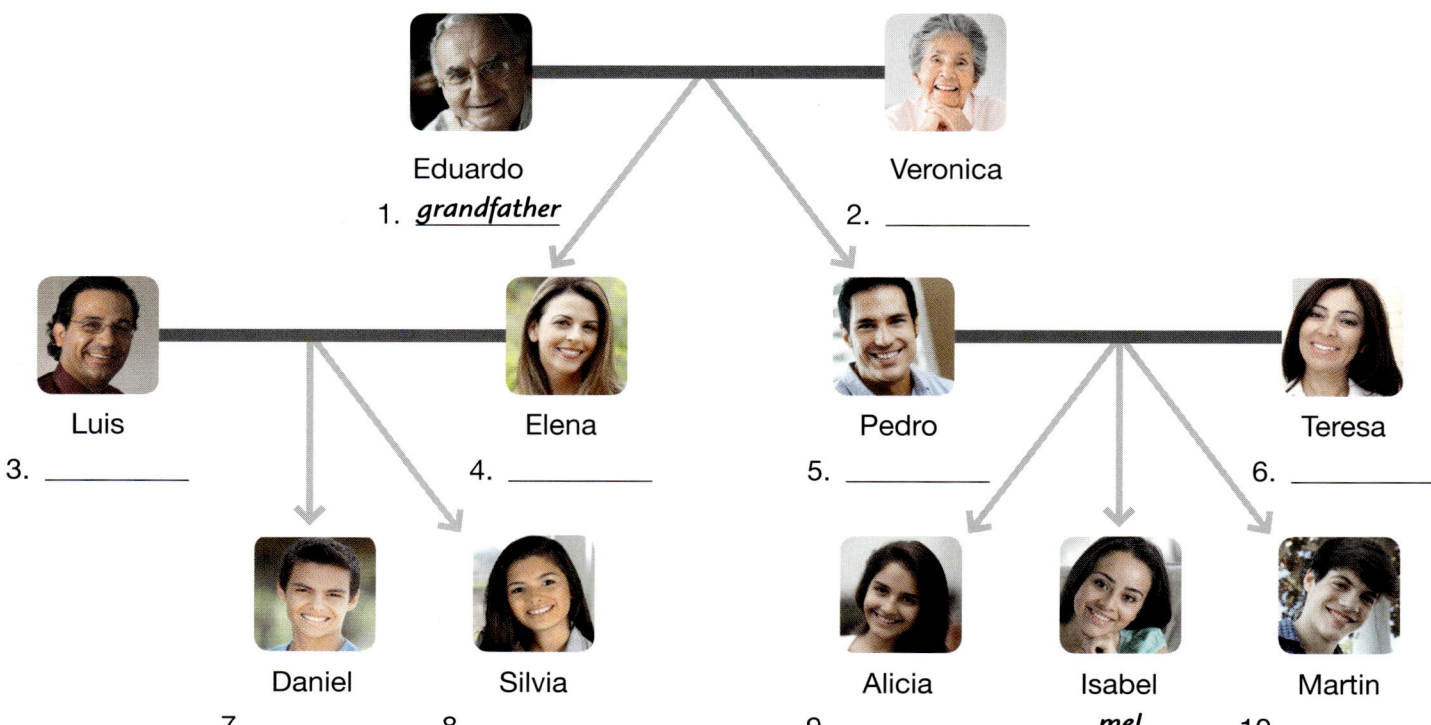

1. *grandfather*
2. _____
3. _____
4. _____
5. _____
6. _____
7. _____
8. _____
9. _____  *me!*  10. _____

**2** Look at Isabel's family tree. Rewrite the sentences to correct the underlined mistakes.

1. Ricardo is Isabel's dad.   *Pedro is Isabel's dad* _____.
2. Teresa is Silvia's uncle.   _____.
3. Eduardo and Veronica are Alicia's cousins.   _____.
4. Elena and Teresa are Martin's sisters.   _____.
5. Veronica is Daniel's mom.   _____.

**3** Circle the correct words to complete the questions and statements.

1. Who **is /(are)** Martin's cousins?
2. His **sister's / sisters'** names are Isabel and Alicia.
3. Pedro is **Silvia's / Silvias'** uncle.
4. What **is / are** their grandmother's name?
5. Her **brother's / brothers'** name is Daniel.
6. Eduardo is **Isabel's / Isabels'** grandfather.
7. Their **parent's / parents'** names are Luis and Elena.

# UNIT 2 WORKBOOK

**4** Complete the mind map. Use the words below.

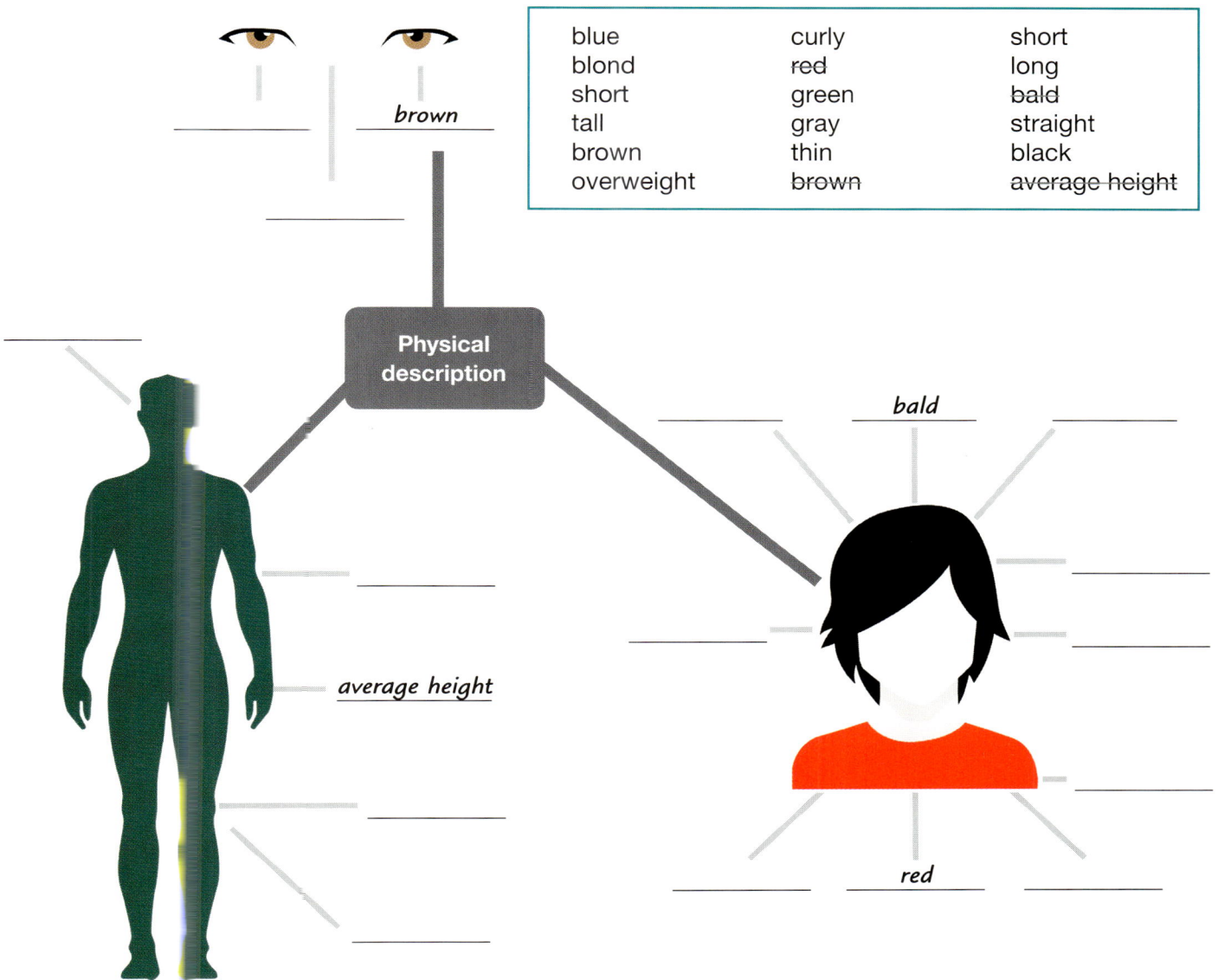

| blue | curly | short |
| blond | red | long |
| short | green | bald |
| tall | gray | straight |
| brown | thin | black |
| overweight | brown | average height |

**5** Circle the correct words to complete the sentences.

1. Rosa's sister **have** / **(has)** long brown hair.
2. We **have** / **has** two uncles and **an** / **the** aunt.
3. He **have** / **has** two brothers. One brother is in Mexico City and the other brother is in Guadalajara. **The** / **A** brother in Mexico City is tall.
4. Victor's sister **have** / **has** green eyes.
5. I **have** / **has** brown eyes and brown hair.
6. They **have** / **has** an aunt, **a** / **an** uncle, and **a** / **an** cousin. Their aunt **have** / **has** curly hair. Their uncle and cousin **have** / **has** straight hair.

# UNIT 3  Where are you from?

**1** Find and circle the countries. Then write the nationality for each country.

| M | E | X | I | C | O | Q | J | K |
|---|---|---|---|---|---|---|---|---|
| H | E | Y | L | A | T | I | D | J |
| A | I | L | A | R | T | S | U | A |
| B | W | Y | R | P | U | L | S | C |
| A | N | I | H | C | A | R | M | J |
| E | I | D | G | I | S | T | E | H |
| B | A | B | R | A | Z | I | L | P |
| Y | P | I | A | J | Y | D | H | F |
| A | S | V | A | Z | G | J | W | T |

**Countries**
1. Brazil
2. Mexico
3. Spain
4. Australia
5. China
6. Italy
7. Peru

**Nationalities**
1. __Brazilian__
2. _____
3. _____
4. _____
5. _____
6. _____
7. _____

**2** Put the letters in order to make geographical feature words.

1. n e o c a          __ocean__
2. a e s f r n o t i r   _____
3. r e s t e d        _____
4. a r a f t w e l l  _____
5. c a b e h          _____
6. t o m n u a n i    _____

**3** Complete the conversation.

**Ana:** Hi. I'm from Mexico. __Where__₁ are you from?

**Tom:** Hi. _____₂ from Canada.

**Ana:** That's interesting! _____₃ it like?

**Tom:** It's big. It _____₄ a lot of mountains and lakes. _____₅ Mexico like?

**Ana:** It's big, too. I'm from the state of Chiapas. It _____₆ mountains, lakes, beaches, and a rainforest.

**Tom:** It sounds beautiful. Is your family in Chiapas now?

**Ana:** No, they _____₇. They're in León and Puebla.

**Tom:** _____₈ in Puebla?

**Ana:** My sister is.

**Tom:** _____₉ she like?

**Ana:** _____₁₀ 19 years old. She _____₁₁ green eyes.

**Tom:** I _____₁₂ a sister, too.

**Ana:** _____₁₃ is she?

**Tom:** _____₁₄ 10 years old.

**Ana:** Really? My brother is 10 years old, too!

## UNIT 3 WORKBOOK

**4** Read about the Huichol and the Zapotec. Check (✓) the correct answers.

The Huichol (or Wixaritari) are an indigenous group. They live in the Sierra Madre mountains. They are originally from San Luis Potosí. They are average height. They have brown eyes and brown hair. They're famous for their beautiful artwork.

The Zapotec are an indigenous group from Oaxaca. The archeological site of Monte Albán is from the Zapotec culture. They are famous for their weaving. Their rugs are beautiful.

1. Who's from the Sierra Madre mountains?
   - [✓] The Huichol
   - [ ] The Zapotec

2. Where are the Huichol originally from?
   - [ ] They're originally from the Sangre de Cristo mountains.
   - [ ] They're originally from San Luis Potosí.

3. Who's from Oaxaca?
   - [ ] The Huichol are from Oaxaca.
   - [ ] The Zapotec are from Oaxaca.

4. Is Monte Albán from the Zapotec or Huichol culture?
   - [ ] It's from the Zapotec culture.
   - [ ] It's from the Huichol culture.

5. What are the Huichol like?
   - [ ] They're average height and they have green eyes and brown hair.
   - [ ] They're average height. They have brown eyes and brown hair.

6. What are the Zapotec famous for?
   - [ ] They're famous for their weaving.
   - [ ] They're famous for their artwork.

**5** Underline the errors. Then rewrite the sentences.

1. What <u>are</u> his name?
   _What is his name_?

2. His name is Cecilia.
   _____.

3. Their names is Cesar and Victor.
   _____.

4. Luis has 16 years old.
   _____.

5. We have a aunt and two cousins.
   _____.

6. Luis have two sisters.
   _____.

7. Cesars' sisters are Silvia and Carmen.
   _____.

8. My brothers have average height.
   _____.

9. Isabel are Chilean.
   _____.

10. Diego is Mexico.
    _____.

31

# SELF-CHECK  UNITS 1–3

## 1 Who's he?

___/6

Read about Liam Hemsworth and complete the sentences.

> Liam Hemsworth is from Australia. He is tall. He has blue eyes and blond hair. Liam is an actor. He's famous for his acting in the movie *The Hunger Games*. He has two brothers. Their names are Chris and Luke. Liam's mother is Leonie. She is a teacher.

1. Liam is from Australia. He's _____ (nationality).
2. Chris is Liam's _____ .
3. Liam's mother _____ a teacher.
4. Liam _____ short.
5. He _____ blue eyes.
6. Liam isn't a teacher. He's _____ actor.

## 2 Questions and answers with the verb *be*

___/6

Match the questions to the correct responses.

1. What's his phone number?  ___
2. Where is she from?  ___
3. You're 16, right?  ___
4. What's your sister like?  ___
5. Is Susana their cousin?  ___
6. Is the waterfall beautiful?  ___

a. She's tall.
b. It's 555–8364.
c. Yes, it is.
d. No, she's not.
e. Yes, I am.
f. She's from Mexico.

## 3 Countries and nationalities

___/6

Write the nationalities.

1. Canada _____
2. Peru _____
3. China _____
4. Spain _____
5. Great Britain _____
6. Brazil _____

## 4 Verbs *be* and *have*

___/7

Complete the conversation with the correct forms of the verbs *be* and *have*.

**Ana:** Who _____ they?
**Paco:** They're my brothers and my sister.
**Ana:** What are their names?
**Paco:** My sister's name _____ Luisa, and my brothers' names are Leo and Joe.
**Ana:** What are they like?
**Paco:** Leo _____ green eyes. Joe and Luisa _____ brown eyes.
**Ana:** _____ your sister tall?
**Paco:** No, she's not. _____ short.
**Ana:** _____ a nice photo.

## Score

Count total points.

Total ___/25

25–23 points Great!   22–20 points Good   19–17 points Needs practice   Below 17 points Ask for help!

# Lifestyles

**UNIT 4 Work and transportation**
▶ I can talk about jobs and work activities.
▶ I can ask and answer questions about transportation.

**UNIT 5 Routines and free time**
▶ I can describe and write about free-time activities.
▶ I can talk and write about my daily routine.

**UNIT 6 Community and culture**
▶ I can talk about places around town.
▶ I can investigate, write, and talk about indigenous cultures.

# UNIT 4 Work and transportation

## 1 Vocabulary  Jobs

**A** 🔊 CD 1:19  Complete the sentences with the words below. Then listen and check your answers.

> student   nurse   musician   ~~chef~~   teach   ~~bring food~~   drive a taxi   answer the phone

1. I ___bring food___.
   I'm a waiter.
2. I _____.
   I'm a receptionist.
3. I play an instrument.
   I'm a _____.
4. I help sick people.
   I'm a _____.

5. I cook food. I'm
   a ___chef___.
6. I _____.
   I'm a teacher.
7. I study. I'm a
   _____.
8. I _____.
   I'm a taxi driver.

**B** Work with a classmate. Talk about the jobs in exercise A. Take turns.

"*I'm a waiter. I bring food.*"

## 2 Language in context  *She answers the phone.*

**A** 🔊 CD 1:20  Listen to people talk about jobs. Circle the jobs. Then check your answers with a classmate.

Susan (cooks) food.
She's a chef.

Luis and Enrique bring food. They're waiters.

Adriana answers the phone.
She's a receptionist.

**B** Work with a classmate. Do you have a job? What is it?

**A:** *I'm a waiter. How about you?*
**B:** *I'm a student.*

## 3 Grammar  CD 1:21

### Simple present

| Simple present | | | |
|---|---|---|---|
| I / You / We / They | cook food. | You / We / They | don't teach. |
| He / She | cooks food. | He / She | doesn't teach. |

**More verbs**

| I / you / we / they | he / she / it |
|---|---|
| I **play** soccer. | He **plays** soccer. |
| I **go** to school. | He **goes** to school. |
| They **teach**. | She **teaches**. |
| You **study**. | She **studies**. |
| We **have** a car. | He **has** a taxi. |

💡 don't = do not    doesn't = does not

**A** Complete the sentences. Then check your answers with a classmate.

1. Nick ___drives___ (drive) a taxi. He ___doesn't drive___ (not / drive) a bus.
2. Elena is a nurse. She _____ (not / teach).
   She _____ (help) sick people.
3. We're students. We _____ (not / cook) food.
   We _____ (study) English.
4. They _____ (have) jobs. They _____ (not / study).
5. You're a musician. You _____ (play) an instrument.
   You _____ (not / answer) the phone.

**B** Work with a classmate. Talk about what you do and don't do. Take turns.

"I don't teach. I study."

## 4 Pronunciation  Third person singular endings

**A**  CD 1:22  Listen and repeat. Notice the sound at the end of the verbs.

Eduardo **answers** the phone.    Luis **helps** people.    Adriana **studies** English.
Felipe **goes** to school.    Ms. Diaz **teaches** my class.    Clara **works**.

**B** Work with a classmate. Say the verbs. Write the verbs in the correct column.

goes    answers    studies    helps    teaches    works

| /s/ sound | /z/ sound | /iz/ sound |
|---|---|---|
|  | goes |  |

▶ Can you talk about jobs and work activities?  ☐ Yes  ☐ No

UNIT 4

35

UNIT 4

## 5 Vocabulary Transportation

**A** 🔊 CD 1:23 Listen and repeat.

walk     ride a bicycle     ride a motorcycle     drive a car

take the subway     take the train     take the bus     take a taxi

**B** Work with a classmate. How do you go to school?

"I walk to school. How about you?"

## 6 Conversation Do you take the bus to school?

**A** 🔊 CD 1:24 Listen.

> **Raul:** Hello. Ana. You're early! Do you take the bus to school?
> **Ana:** Hi, Raul. No, I don't. I ride a bicycle.
> **Raul:** Wow! That's cool.
> **Ana:** What about you? Do you take the bus to school?
> **Raul:** No, I don't. I walk and I take the subway.

**B** Practice the conversation with a classmate.

UNIT 4

## 7 Grammar 🔊 CD 1:25

**Simple present *yes / no* questions**

**Do** you **walk** to work?
Yes, I **do**. / No, I **don't**.

**Does** Raul **ride** a motorcycle?
Yes, he **does**. / No, he **doesn't**.

**Do** you and your family **take** the bus?
Yes, we **do**. / No, we **don't**.

**Do** your friends **ride** bicycles?
Yes, they **do**. / No, they **don't**.

**A** Write questions with the information below. Then check your questions with a classmate.

1. (take a taxi / you / to school / Do) *Do you take a taxi to school* ?
2. (your best friend / Does / ride / a motorcycle) _____?
3. (the bus / you and your friends / Do / take) _____?
4. (your cousin / Does / take the subway) _____?
5. (Do / a bicycle / ride / you) _____?

**B** Work with a classmate. Ask and answer the questions. Use your own information. Take turns.

**A:** *Do you take a taxi to school?*
**B:** *No, I don't. I walk.*

## 8 Speaking  Transportation interview

**A** Write your name and check (✓) the transportation you use. Ask two classmates for their information. Complete the chart.

| Transportation | Carmen | Me | Name: _____ | Name: _____ |
|---|---|---|---|---|
| ride a bicycle | ✓ | | | |
| take a taxi | ✓ | | | |
| take the subway | ✗ | | | |
| take the bus | ✗ | | | |
| walk | ✓ | | | |
| take the train | ✗ | | | |

**B** Work with a different classmate. Look at the chart. Talk about the transportation other students use and don't use.

*"Ricardo walks to school. He doesn't ride a bicycle. Vero takes the bus. They don't take the train."*

▶ Can you ask and answer questions about transportation?   ☐ Yes  ☐ No

# UNIT 5 Routines and free time

## 1 Vocabulary  Activities and sports

**A** 🔊 CD 1:26  Listen and repeat.

### Activities

go shopping      listen to music      text friends

hang out      play computer games      watch TV

### Sports

do karate      do gymnastics      go swimming      play soccer      play basketball

**B** Work with a classmate. What activities and sports do you do?

"I listen to music, and I play soccer. What about you?"

## 2 Language in context  *He sometimes listens to music.*

**A** 🔊 CD 1:27  Read about what Andrew and Grace do. Underline activities. Circle sports. Then check your answers with a classmate.

Andrew does (karate).
He sometimes <u>listens to music</u>.

Grace often plays computer games with friends. She also goes swimming.

**B** Work with a classmate. What do you and your family do in your free time?

"I play basketball. My sister does gymnastics."

## 3 Grammar  CD 1:28

**Adverbs of frequency; *ever***

| | |
|---|---|
| I **always** take the bus to school. 100% | Do you **ever** play basketball? |
| She **usually** does karate. | Yes, I do. I usually play after school. |
| He **often** hangs out with his friends. | |
| We **sometimes** go shopping. | No, I never play basketball. / |
| You **hardly ever** play the guitar. | No, I don't. |
| They **never** play basketball. 0% | |

**A** Write questions. Then check your questions with a classmate.

1. you text your friends — *Do you ever text your friends*?
2. you play soccer — _____?
3. you listen to music — _____?
4. you hang out with friends — _____?
5. you go swimming — _____?
6. you watch TV — _____?

**B** Work with a classmate. Ask and answer the questions. Take turns.

**A:** *Do you ever text your friends?*
**B:** *Yes, I do sometimes. How about you?*

## 4 Speaking   My free time

**A** Complete the chart with free time activities. Use your own information.

| I usually ... | I sometimes ... | I never ... |
|---|---|---|
| watch TV after school. | | |

**B** Work in a small group. Talk about what you do in your free time.

**A:** *I never go swimming.*
**B:** *Really? I do sometimes. I never play computer games.*

▶ Can you describe and write about free time activities?   ☐ Yes   ☐ No

# UNIT 5

## 5 Vocabulary  Days of the week and routines

**A** CD 1:29  Listen and repeat.

| Sunday | Monday | Tuesday | Wednesday | Thursday | Friday | Saturday |

- get up
- take a shower
- eat breakfast
- go to school
- study
- exercise
- do homework
- eat dinner
- check email
- go to bed

**B** Work with a classmate. Which activities do you do?

**A:** *I take a shower. I . . . .*
**B:** *I exercise. I . . . .*

## 6 Conversation  *What do you do every morning?*

**A** CD 1:30  Listen.

**Jorge:** What do you do every morning?
**Vero:** I always get up and take a shower.
**Jorge:** When do you go to school?
**Vero:** I go to school after I eat breakfast.
**Jorge:** What do you usually do on the weekends?
**Vero:** I usually watch TV. Sometimes I ride my bike. How about you?
**Jorge:** Me too! I watch TV and hang out.
**Vero:** Really? Who do you hang out with?
**Jorge:** Usually with my brother and our friends.

**B** Practice the conversation with a classmate.

## 7 Grammar 🔊 CD 1:31
**Simple present *Wh-* questions, *How often...?*, and *time expressions***

### Wh- questions

**What do** you do in your free time?
I play soccer.

**Where does** she do karate?
In the gym.

**How do** they get home?
They take the bus.

**Who does** he play soccer with?
He plays with his friends.

**When do** you usually check your email?
I usually check my email in the evenings.

**How often** does she do karate?
She does karate **on Tuesdays and Thursdays**.

### Time expressions

***on*** + Mondays, Tuesdays, Wednesdays, Thursdays, Fridays, Saturdays, Sundays
***on*** + the weekends / week days
***in*** + the mornings, the afternoons, the evenings
***every day*; *at night***

**A** Answer the questions  Use your own information. Then check your answers with a classmate.

1. What do you eat for breakfast? *I usually eat cereal* _____.
2. How often do you go to your grandparents' house? _____
_____.
3. Where do you go in the afternoon? _____.
4. When do you go to English class? _____.
5. Who do you see on the weekends? _____.
6. How do you get to school? _____.

**B** Work with a classmate. Ask and answer the questions. Take turns.

**A:** *What do you eat for breakfast?*
**B:** *I usually eat granola and fruit. What do you eat for breakfast?*

## 8 Speaking   My daily routine

**A** Write about your daily routine.

> *I get up and I take a shower. Then I listen to music and I eat ...*

**B** Work in a small group. Present your daily routine. Listen to classmates' presentations. Evaluate them. Use the peer evaluation form on page 46.

▶ Can you talk and write about your daily routine?   ☐ Yes  ☐ No

# UNIT 6 Community and culture

## 1 Vocabulary  Places around town

**A** 🔊 CD 1:32 Write the words under the pictures. Then listen and check your answers.

> restaurant    ~~park~~    mall    ~~internet café~~    movies / movie theater    gym

1. _park_
2. _____
3. _____
4. _____
5. _internet café_
6. _____

**B** Work with a classmate. What places do you like?

"I like the mall. How about you?"

## 2 Language in context  *Leon always goes to the movies on the weekend.*

**A** 🔊 CD 1:33 Listen. Circle the places around town. Underline the activities. Then check your answers with a classmate.

Alicia often <u>checks her email</u> at the (internet café) on Saturday afternoons.

Luis usually plays soccer in the park on Saturday mornings.

Leon always goes to the movies on the weekend.

**B** Work with a classmate. Where do you go on the weekends?

"I usually go to my grandparents' house on the weekends."

42

UNIT 6

## 3 Grammar 🔊 CD 1:34

**Prepositions of location**

| go + to | other verbs + at / in |
|---|---|
| go **to** the movies | go shopping **at / in** the mall |
| go **to** the mall | check email **at / in** an internet café |
| go **to** the park | exercise **at / in** the gym |
| go **to** the café | play soccer **at / in** the park |
| go **to** school | watch TV **at** home |

💡 We watch TV **at** home, NOT **in** home

We go **to** school, NOT **to the** school

**A** Complete the sentences with *to*, *at*, or *in*. Then check your answers with a classmate.

1. Do you ever go ___to___ the mall?
2. Sam usually plays soccer _____ the park.
3. José often checks his email _____ an internet café.
4. They go _____ the movies every weekend.
5. Bella exercises _____ the gym.

**B** Work with a classmate. Ask and answer questions. Where do you do these activities? Take turns.

**A:** *Where do you check your email?*
**B:** *I check my email at home. How about you?*

## 4 Speaking  E-pal / classmate interview

**A** Complete the chart with your information. Then interview your e-pal / classmate and write the information in the chart.

| Questions | My information | My e-pal / my classmate |
|---|---|---|
| What do you do on weekends? | I sometimes go to the movies. | |
| Do you ever go shopping? | | |
| Where do you exercise? | | |
| How often do you check your email? | | |
| When do you go to the movies? | | |
| Do you often go to restaurants? | | |

**B** Work in a small group. Present your information.

"*My e-pal / classmate is Leticia Alvarez. She is from Puebla. She goes to the gym on the weekends ...*"

▶ Can you talk about places around town?  ☐ Yes  ☐ No

# UNIT 6

## 5 Reading  The Otomí and the Cora

**A** Read about two indigenous cultures. Circle where the Otomí and Cora people come from. Then check your answers with a classmate.

The Otomí people are from central Mexico, the Valle del Mezquital. They speak a language called Otomí. They prepare good food. The Otomí make beautiful textiles.

The Cora people live in the Sierra Madre, in Nayarit. They speak the Cora language. Some Cora people are musicians. They play instruments. The Cora people like music!

**B** Answer the questions. Then check your answers with a classmate.

1. What language do the Otomí people speak? _They speak Otomí_____.
2. Where do the Cora people live? _____.
3. What do the Otomí people make? _____.
4. What do the Cora people play? _____.

## 6 Listening  The famous Triqui basketball players!

**A**  🔊 CD 1:35  Listen to a description of a basketball team. Check (✓) the correct picture of the team.

**B**  🔊 CD 1:36  Listen again. Circle T (true) or F (false). Then check your answers with a classmate.

The Triqui boys:
1. ... are from Jalisco.                    T    (F)
2. ... play basketball at school.           T    F
3. ... play basketball with shoes.          T    F

UNIT 6

## 7 Writing Indigenous groups

**A** Work in a group. Choose an indigenous group from the list. Research the group and complete the questionnaire.

> The Náhuas    The Mixtec    The Tzeltal    The Purépecha

**Name of indigenous group:**

**Where do they come from?**

**What language do they speak?**

**What do they eat?**

**What do they do in their free time?**

**What sports do they play?**

**B** Work in a group. Write a presentation. Use complete sentences.

_The Náhuas are from ..._

## 8 Speaking Class presentation

**A** Work in a group. Practice your presentation. Record it.

"The Náhuas are from ..."

**B** Present your recording to another group. Listen to your classmates' recordings. Evaluate them. Use the peer evaluation form on page 46.

▶ Can you investigate, write, and talk about indigenous cultures?
☐ Yes    ☐ No

# PEER EVALUATION  UNITS 4–6

## UNIT 5  page 41, exercise 8B  Speaking My daily routine

Listen to your classmates talking about their daily routine.
Evaluate the presentations. Write their scores.

**Score key**
3 = Great!   2 = Good   1 = Needs practice

| I am evaluating: | Grammar<br>uses the simple present correctly | Vocabulary<br>uses time expressions (*on Mondays, in the mornings, on the weekends*) and routine words accurately | Fluency<br>speaks clearly and naturally | Total |
|---|---|---|---|---|
| 1. | | | | /9 |
| 2. | | | | /9 |
| 3. | | | | /9 |
| 4. | | | | /9 |

## UNIT 6  page 45, exercise 8B  Speaking Class presentation

Listen to your classmates' recordings about indigenous cultures.
Evaluate the presentations. Write their scores.

**Score key**
3 = Great!   2 = Good   1 = Needs practice

| I am evaluating: | Grammar<br>uses the simple present correctly | Vocabulary<br>uses free-time activities, food and sports words accurately | Fluency<br>speaks clearly and naturally | Total |
|---|---|---|---|---|
| 1. | | | | /9 |
| 2. | | | | /9 |
| 3. | | | | /9 |
| 4. | | | | /9 |

## UNIT 4–6  Study cards

Look at your classmates' study cards. Evaluate them. Write their scores.

**Score key**
3 = Great!   2 = Good   1 = Needs practice

| I am evaluating: | work activities | sport activities | community activities | free-time activities | places around town | Total |
|---|---|---|---|---|---|---|
| 1. | | | | | | /15 |
| 2. | | | | | | /15 |
| 3. | | | | | | /15 |
| 4. | | | | | | /15 |

# SELF EVALUATION  UNITS 4–6

Read the sentences. Write your score for each.

**Score key**
**3** = I can do this very well   **2** = I can do this   **1** = I need more practice

| What I can do | Score |
|---|---|
| 1. I can talk about jobs and work activities.<br>*Lisa helps people. She's a nurse.* | |
| 2. I can ask and answer questions about transportation.<br>*Do you take the bus to school?*<br>*No, I don't. I walk to school.* | |
| 3. I can describe and write about free-time activities.<br>*I sometimes go shopping. We always text our friends.* | |
| 4. I can talk and write about my daily routine.<br>*I get up early and take a shower. I usually eat fruit for breakfast.*<br>*I exercise at the gym in the afternoons.* | |
| 5. I can talk about places around town.<br>*I often check email at the internet café.*<br>*Sometimes I go to the movies.* | |
| 6. I can investigate, write, and talk about indigenous cultures.<br>*The Náhuas are from central Mexico.*<br>*They speak a language called Náhuatl.* | |
| Total | |

# UNIT 4 Work and transportation

**1** Write the jobs under the correct pictures.

| teacher | waiter | receptionist | chef |
| nurse | ~~taxi driver~~ | musician | student |

Billy
1. _taxi driver_

Carmen
2. _____

Peter
3. _____

Vero
4. _____

Antonio
5. _____

Lety
6. _____

Jacob
7. _____

Ana
8. _____

**2** Write two sentences for each person in exercise 1. Write what their jobs are and what they do.

| ~~drive a taxi~~ | play an instrument | cook food | study |
| answer the phone | teach | help sick people | bring food |

1. Billy       _He's a taxi driver. He drives a taxi._
2. Carmen   _____
3. Peter     _____
4. Vero      _____
5. Antonio   _____
6. Lety      _____
7. Jacob     _____
8. Ana       _____

## UNIT 4 WORKBOOK

**3** Put the letters of each word in order. Then complete the crossword.

Across →
3. ITAX
6. RAC
7. YBUSWA
8. KWAL

Down ↓
1. ELYCCTORMO
2. CYBILEC
4. USB
5. RIANT

**4** Circle the verbs to make transportation phrases. Then write the phrases.

1. (take) / walk / have the subway      _take the subway_
2. walk / have / ride a motorcycle      _____
3. drive / have / ride a car            _____
4. have / drive / take the bus          _____
5. drive / ride / walk a bicycle        _____
6. have / ride / take a taxi            _____

**5** Complete the conversations with the simple present forms of the verbs.

1. **Cecy:** ____Do____ you ____have____ (have) a car, Luis?
   **Luis:** No, I _____. I _____ (walk) to school.
2. **Laura:** Ashley and Madison _____ (ride) their bicycles to school.
   **Daniel:** _____ they _____ (take) the bus, too?
   **Laura:** Yes, they _____!
3. **Lety:** _____ Eduardo _____ (drive) a car to school?
   **Carlos:** No, he _____. He _____ (ride) a bicycle.
4. **Allison:** _____ you _____ (play) the piano?
   **James:** No, I _____, but my sister _____.
5. **Emilio:** _____ your brothers _____ work?
   **Nancy:** Yes, they _____. Arturo _____ (drive) a taxi. Cesar _____ (cook) food at a restaurant.
6. **Roger:** _____ your mom _____ (teach) English?
   **Karen:** No, she _____. She _____ (teach) math.

# UNIT 5  Routines and free time

**1** Look at the chart. Then complete the sentences. Use the simple present.

|  | hang out with friends | watch TV | play computer games | do gymnastics | go swimming | play basketball | listen to music | do karate | go shopping |
|---|---|---|---|---|---|---|---|---|---|
| Rafa |  |  |  | ✓ |  |  |  |  |  |
| Cesar |  |  |  |  |  |  | ✓ |  |  |
| Ana | ✓ |  |  |  |  |  |  |  |  |
| Eva |  |  |  |  |  |  |  |  | ✓ |
| Gaby |  |  |  |  | ✓ |  |  |  |  |
| Jorge |  |  |  |  |  | ✓ |  |  |  |
| Alicia |  | ✓ |  |  |  |  |  |  |  |
| Pedro |  |  |  |  |  |  |  | ✓ |  |

1. Rafa *does gymnastics* .
2. Cesar _____ .
3. Ana _____ .
4. Eva _____ .
5. Gaby _____ .
6. Jorge _____ .
7. Alicia _____ .
8. Pedro _____ .

**2** Use the adverbs of frequency and the correct form of the verbs in parentheses to complete the conversations.

1. **A:** Do you _____*ever go*_____ (ever / go) shopping?
   **B:** Yes, I _____ . I _____ (sometimes / go) shopping with my mother.

2. **A:** Does Manuel _____ (ever / play) basketball?
   **B:** He _____ (hardly ever / play) basketball, but he _____ (often / do) karate.

3. **A:** _____ Emily _____ (ever / text) her friends?
   **B:** Yes, she _____ . She _____ (often / text) her friends after school.

4. **A:** _____ Josh and Alex _____ (ever / watch) TV?
   **B:** No, they _____ . They _____ (never / watch) TV.

5. **A:** _____ Carmen _____ (ever / go) swimming on Mondays?
   **B:** No, she _____ . She _____ (never / go) swimming on Mondays.

6. **A:** _____ you _____ (ever / do) karate?
   **B:** Yes, I _____ (usually / do) karate on weekends.

# UNIT 5 WORKBOOK

**3** Write the days of the week in the correct order.

_Sunday_ _____ _Monday_ _____ _____ _____

_____ _____ _____

**4** Complete the sentences about Ricardo's routine. Use the days of the week and the pictures in exercise 3.

1. Ricardo _studies on Sundays_ _____.
2. Ricardo _____ early _____.
3. Ricardo _____.
4. Ricardo _____.
5. Ricardo _____ with his family _____.
6. Ricardo _____ _____.
7. Ricardo _____ in the park _____.

**5** Complete the questions with *wh-* question words.

1. **A:** _____Who_____ does Santiago walk to school with?
   **B:** Santiago walks to school with Vera.
2. **A:** _____ do you watch TV, Alicia?
   **B:** I watch TV in the evenings.
3. **A:** _____ does Emiliano exercise?
   **B:** Emiliano exercises every day.
4. **A:** _____ does Eduardo do karate?
   **B:** Eduardo does karate in the park.
5. **A:** _____ does David do on Thursdays?
   **B:** David plays soccer on Thursdays.
6. **A:** _____ do they get to the park?
   **B:** They ride their bicycles to the park.
7. **A:** _____ plays the guitar in your family?
   **B:** _____.

# UNIT 6 Community and culture

**1** Find and circle the places. Use the words below.

| restaurant | park | mall | café | movies | ~~gym~~ |

| R | C | E | M | Z | G | I | E | S | Z |
|---|---|---|---|---|---|---|---|---|---|
| C | E | Q | T | Y | T | P | U | J | A |
| A | P | S | M | Y | M | A | L | L | S |
| F | C | A | T | S | E | I | V | O | M |
| E | P | X | R | A | R | X | J | K | Z |
| S | Y | A | S | K | U | C | I | K | W |
| W | N | O | R | G | N | R | O | B | A |
| L | G | T | C | K | N | Z | A | H | T |
| G | F | I | S | N | K | C | W | N | W |
| Y | D | E | Z | T | L | D | Q | Q | T |

**2** Complete the sentences. Use the words from exercise 1.

1. I exercise at the _____*gym*_____ every morning.
2. On weekends, we sometimes eat in a _____.
3. Arturo checks email at the internet _____.
4. Miguel and Eduardo often play soccer in the _____.
5. Lety goes shopping in the _____ every Saturday.
6. We go to the _____ on the weekends.

**3** Circle the correct words to complete the sentences.

1. I like to go **to** / at  the park in the afternoons.
2. Do you check your email  **to / at**  the internet café?
3. We exercise **to / in**  the gym.
4. I go  **to / at** the mall on Sundays.
5. We eat **to / in**  a restaurant on Friday evenings.
6. She goes **to / in**  the movies with her friends on Saturdays.
7. They go **to / at**  school on weekdays.
8. He likes to eat dinner **to / at**  home.

52  Unit 6 Workbook

# UNIT 6 WORKBOOK

**4** Read about the Purépecha and the Maya. Check the correct answers.

The Purépecha of Michoacán are an indigenous group from central Mexico. The Purépecha language is called Purépecha. The Purépecha people like music and make guitars. They sing songs about daily life.

The Maya are an indigenous group from the Yucatán peninsula. They speak Maya and Spanish. The Maya are famous for the great city of Chichén Itzá. They make beautiful clothes.

1. Who is from central Mexico?
   - [ ] The Maya
   - [✓] The Purépecha

2. Who is famous for one of their cities?
   - [ ] The Purépecha
   - [ ] The Maya

3. Who is from Yucatán?
   - [ ] The Maya are from Yucatán.
   - [ ] The Purépecha are from Yucatán.

4. What do the Purépecha sing about?
   - [ ] They sing about cities.
   - [ ] They sing about daily life.

5. What do the Maya make?
   - [ ] They make guitars.
   - [ ] They make beautiful clothes.

6. What do the Purépecha like?
   - [ ] They like music.
   - [ ] They like clothes.

**5** Underline the errors. Rewrite the sentences.

1. We <u>doesn't</u> drive a car.
   _We don't drive a car_.

2. I get up early at the mornings
   _____.

3. Who Enrique plays soccer with?
   _____?

4. I takes the train.
   _____.

5. <u>What you do</u> in your free time?
   _What do you do in your free time_?

6. Javier is a student. He study.
   _____.

7. You walks to work?
   _____?

8. We go at the movies on weekends.
   _____.

9. Do ever you check your email?
   _____?

10. Isabel have a motorcycle.
    _____.

53

# SELF-CHECK  UNITS 4–6

## 1 Living and working      /6
Read about Jorge and Silvia and complete the sentences.

> Jorge is a musician. He plays the guitar. Jorge walks to work. Sometimes he rides his bicycle to the park. Jorge's friend is Silvia. She likes music, but she doesn't play an instrument. She's a nurse. She helps people. She doesn't walk to work. She takes the bus.

1. Silva _____ a musician.
2. Jorge _____ the bus to work. He walks.
3. Silvia _____ the bus to work.
4. Silvia _____ music.
5. Silvia _____ a job. She's a nurse.
6. Jorge sometimes rides his _____.

## 2 Questions with *do* or *does*      /6
Put the words in order to make questions. Use *do* or *does*.

1. when / you / study
2. how often / Ashley / play / the piano
3. ever / he / to school / walk
4. your parents / eat out / ever
5. where / the chef / cook / food
6. what / class / she / teach

## 3 Routines and activities      /13
Complete the sentences and questions with the correct forms of the verbs.

| take | play | watch TV | exercise | get up | eat |
| do | go shopping | hang out | check | ride | |

1. I usually _____ at 5 a.m.
2. I always _____ a shower and then I _____ breakfast.
3. He _____ the bus to school. He doesn't walk.
4. I _____ computer games or I _____ with my friends in my free time.
5. When do you _____ email?
6. We usually _____ at the mall. Sometimes we go to my house and _____.
7. She _____ a bicycle to school. She takes the bus.
8. No, I _____ any sports, but my sister often _____ karate!
9. Does she ever _____ at the gym?

## Score
Count total points.      Total ___/25

**25–23 points** Great!   **22–20 points** Good   **19–17 points** Needs practice   **Below 17 points** Ask for help!

# Our activities

**UNIT 7  Our day**
- I can ask for and tell the time.
- I can talk about jobs and work activities.

**UNIT 8  What's happening?**
- I can talk about activities people are doing right now.
- I can describe online activities and daily routines.

**UNIT 9  Our society**
- I can talk about social issues.
- I can write and perform a rap about social issues.

# UNIT 7 Our day

## 1 Vocabulary  Telling the time

**A** CD 2:02  Listen and repeat.

It's five o'clock.

It's noon.
It's twelve p.m.

It's midnight.
It's twelve a.m.

It's half past four.
It's four thirty.

It's a quarter to two.
It's one forty-five.

It's twenty to three.
It's two forty.

It's ten-oh-five.
It's five after ten.

It's a quarter after six.
It's six fifteen.

**B** Work with a classmate. Point to pictures from exercise A. Ask and answer questions about the time. Take turns.

A: *What's the time in this picture?*
B: *It's half past four. / It's four thirty.*

## 2 Language in context  What time is it?

**A** CD 2:03  Listen to people ask about the time. Underline the times. Then check your answers with a classmate.

**Joe:** Excuse me. What time is it?
**Emma:** It's <u>half past seven</u>.
**Joe:** Oh no! I'm late!

**Naomi:** What time do you eat dinner?
**Javier:** We usually eat dinner at eight o'clock.

**David:** What time do you go to bed?
**Lisa:** I usually go to bed at a quarter to ten.

**B** Work with a classmate. Ask and answer the questions. Use your own information. Take turns.

A: *What time do you eat dinner?*
B: *I eat dinner at seven thirty.*

56

## 3 Grammar  CD 2:04 — Review of simple present *Wh-* questions

**When** do you have lunch?
I have lunch **at 2 p.m.**

**What time** do you go to bed?
I go to bed **at half past ten.**

**What time** is it?
It's **one fifteen.**

**What** does he do on Saturdays?
He **plays soccer.**

**Where** does he play soccer?
He plays soccer **in the park.**

**Who** does he see in the park?
He sees **his friends.**

**A** Read the answers. Write the question for each answer. Then check your answers with a classmate.

1. **A:** We go to the mall on the weekends. (where)
   **B:** _Where do you go on the weekends_?

2. **A:** I go to school at 6:30 a.m. (what time)
   **B:** _____?

3. **A:** I watch TV in the evenings. (when)
   **B:** _____?

4. **A:** He usually eats a sandwich for lunch. (what)
   **B:** _____?

5. **A:** My teacher sees students every day. (who)
   **B:** _____?

**B** Work with a classmate. Ask and answer the questions in exercise A. Use your own information.

**A:** *Where do you go on the weekends?*
**B:** *I usually go to the movies.*

## 4 Pronunciation  Reduction of *to*

**A**  CD 2:05  Listen and repeat. Notice how *to* sounds.

- It's ten to two.
- It's twenty-five to one.
- It's a quarter to seven.

**B** Work with a classmate. Practice saying the times. Use the reduced form of *to*.

- It's five to one.
- It's ten to three.
- It's a quarter to five.
- It's twenty to nine.

▶ Can you ask for and tell the time?  ☐ Yes  ☐ No

UNIT 7

## 5 Vocabulary  More jobs

**A** 🔊 CD 2:06  Complete the sentences with the words below. Then listen and check your answers.

> ~~driver~~   electrician   singer   accountant   ~~doctor~~   pilot   ~~flight attendant~~   police officer

  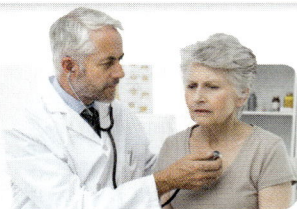 

1. A _flight attendant_ helps passengers.
2. A _____ responds to emergencies.
3. A _doctor_ sees patients.
4. A _____ flies an airplane.

5. An _____ works with numbers.
6. A _____ sings songs.
7. An _____ fixes electrical problems.
8. A _driver_ drives a car.

**B** Work with a classmate. What do the people in the photos do?

**A:** What does a doctor do?
**B:** A doctor sees patients.

## 6 Conversation  I'm reading about jobs.

**A** 🔊 CD 2:07  Listen.

**Pedro:** What are you doing, Jessica?
**Jessica:** I'm reading about jobs at an airport. This is a flight attendant. She's helping passengers.
**Pedro:** Oh, yeah. That's a pilot. He's flying the plane.
**Jessica:** Yeah. That's a cool job!
**Pedro:** How about this guy? What's he doing?
**Jessica:** He's a driver. He's waiting for passengers.

**B** Practice the conversation with a classmate.

## 7 Grammar 🔊 CD 2:08

### Present continuous

| | |
|---|---|
| I'm **reading** about jobs. | I'm **not writing** about jobs. |
| He's **fixing** the airplane. | He's **not flying** the airplane. |
| She's **listening** to a song. | She's **not singing** a song. |
| We're **studying** English. | We're **not studying** French. |
| They're **walking** to school. | They're **not driving** to school. |

**A** Complete the conversations with the present continuous form of the verbs. Then check your answers with a classmate.

1. *I'm listening* to the radio. (I / listen)
2. _____ dinner now. (He / eat)
3. _____ to school. (They / not / walk)
4. _____ food to people in the café. (She / bring)
5. _____ chemistry. (You / not / study)
6. _____ in the park. (They / exercise)

**B** Work with a classmate. Say two things that you're doing now and two things that you're not doing now. Take turns.

**A:** *I'm not walking to school. I'm studying English.*
**B:** *I'm not listening to music. I'm talking to you.*

## 8 Speaking  Act it out!

**A** Make a list of activities.

| *fly an airplane* | *eat an apple* |
|---|---|
| _____ | _____ |
| _____ | _____ |
| _____ | _____ |

**B** Work in a small group. Perform an action. Your classmates guess what you are doing. Take turns.

**A:** *You're flying an airplane!*
**B:** *No! You're driving a car!*

▶ Can you talk about jobs and work activities?   ☐ Yes   ☐ No

# UNIT 8 What's happening?

## 1 Vocabulary  Clothing and colors

**A** 🔊 CD 2:09  Listen and repeat.

blue top / black pants

red sweater

pink dress

green jacket / white shirt

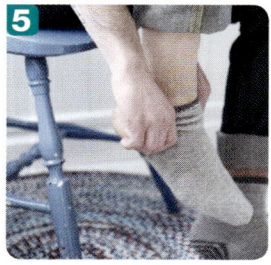
gray socks

brown jacket / yellow skirt

purple shoes

orange shorts

**B** Work with a classmate. Point to pictures in exercise A. Ask and answer questions. Take turns.

**A:** What is she wearing in this picture?   **B:** She's wearing a pink dress.

## 2 Language in context  Is Ana watching a movie?

**A** 🔊 CD 2:10  Listen to questions about what people are doing or wearing. Underline the actions. Then check your answers with a classmate.

Is Ana <u>watching</u> a movie?
No, she isn't. She's playing computer games.

Is Patricia wearing a dress?
No, she isn't. She's wearing jeans.

Is Ricardo reading?
Yes, he is. He's studying for a test.

**B** Work with a classmate. Say what other classmates are doing or wearing. Take turns.

*"Arturo isn't watching a movie. He's talking to Luis."*

## 3 Grammar  CD 2:11

**Present continuous *yes / no* questions**

| | |
|---|---|
| **Am** I **wearing** your sweater? | Yes, **you are**. / No, **you're not**. |
| **Are** you **watching** TV? | Yes, **I am**. / No, **I'm not**. |
| **Is** she **reading** a book? | Yes, **she is**. / No, **she's not**. |
| **Are** we **having** pizza for lunch? | Yes, **we are**. / No, **we're not**. |
| **Are** they **eating** dinner? | Yes, **they are**. / No, **they're not**. |

**A** Write the questions. Then check your questions with a classmate.

1. wearing / are / black / you / shoes — *Are you wearing black shoes* ?
2. shirts / we / wearing / white / are _____?
3. is / a book / reading / teacher / your _____?
4. best friend / is / breakfast / your / eating _____?
5. watching / are / a movie / your / classmates _____?
6. an airplane / I / am / flying _____?

**B** Work with a classmate. Ask and answer the questions. Use your own information. Take turns.

A: *Are you wearing black shoes?*
B: *Yes, I am.*

## 4 Speaking  Our class closet!

**A** Write the color of your favorite clothes in the chart.

| Clothing | Me | Name: _____ | Name: _____ |
|---|---|---|---|
| pants | blue | | |
| sweater | | | |
| socks | | | |
| shirt | | | |
| shoes | | | |

**B** Work with two classmates. Write their names in the chart. Ask questions about the color of their favorite clothes. Take turns.

A: *Is your favorite sweater black?*
B: *No, it isn't. It's green.*

▶ Can you talk about activities people are doing right now?  ☐ Yes  ☐ No

## 5 Vocabulary  Online activities

**A** 🔊 CD 2:12  Listen and repeat.

1. They're chatting online.
2. He's checking email.
3. She's surfing the Internet.
4. We're downloading movies.

  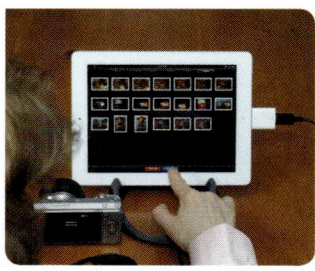 

5. She's posting a message.
6. We're shopping online.
7. You're uploading pictures.
8. I'm reading news reports.

**B** Work with a classmate. Point to the people in the pictures in exercise A. Ask your classmate what they are doing. Take turns.

**A:** *Is he shopping online in this picture?*
**B:** *No, he isn't. He's checking email.*

## 6 Conversation  *What's she doing?*

**A** 🔊 CD 2:13  Listen.

| | |
|---|---|
| **Carlos:** | *What are you doing?* |
| **Karina:** | *I'm chatting with friends online. What about you?* |
| **Carlos:** | *I'm checking email.* |
| **Karina:** | *Hey! Where's Monica?* |
| **Carlos:** | *She's at home.* |
| **Karina:** | *What's she doing?* |
| **Carlos:** | *She's downloading movies.* |

**B** Practice the conversation with a classmate.

## 7 Grammar 🔊 CD 2:14

**Present continuous with Wh- questions**

What**'s** Karen **watching**?
She's watching a movie.

What **are** William and Jorge **doing**?
They're chatting online.

Who**'s talking** on the radio?
The Governor is talking on the radio.

Where **are** you **going**?
We're going to the cafeteria.

**A** Complete the questions with the correct Wh- question words and form of the verb be. Then check your answers with a classmate.

1. _What are_ you doing now? — I'm answering these questions.
2. _____ the teacher doing? — She's helping students.
3. _____ you wearing? — I'm wearing a blue sweater.
4. _____ you sitting? — I'm sitting with my friends.
5. _____ studying English? — We're studying English.

**B** Work with a classmate. Ask and answer the questions in exercise A. Use your own information. Take turns.

**A:** What's the teacher doing?
**B:** He's writing on the board.

## 8 Speaking It's Saturday!

**A** Today is Saturday. What are you doing? Complete the chart with your own information.

| It's Saturday afternoon | Me | Name: _____ |
|---|---|---|
| Where are you going? | to the baseball game | |
| Who are you seeing? | | |
| What are you doing? | | |
| What are you wearing? | | |

**B** Work with a classmate. Today is Saturday. Ask the questions. Write what your classmate is doing. Take turns.

**A:** Where are you going?
**B:** I'm going to the baseball game.

▶ Can you describe online activities and daily routines?  ☐ Yes  ☐ No

# UNIT 9 Our society

## 1 Vocabulary  Cyber bullying

**A** CD 2:15  Look at the words and their definitions. Listen and repeat.

### Acts of cyber bullying

- spreading rumors → saying things that are not true
- making hurtful comments → saying mean things to someone
- pretending to be someone else → acting like you are someone else online
- posting embarrassing pictures → uploading humiliating pictures of someone

### Solutions

- ignore (the bully) → do not answer bullying messages or texts
- collect evidence → create an archive of bullying messages
- report threats → tell your parents, a teacher, or another adult
- block email and cell phone → prevent communication from the bully
- spend time doing things you like → do things you enjoy with family and friends
- share feelings → talk about how you feel

**B** Work with a classmate. Look at the solutions. Which solution do you think is very important?

*"I think it's important to tell your family."*

## 2 Language in context  *We don't have time for cyber bullying!*

**A** CD 2:16  Listen to students talk about cyber bullying.

My friends and I don't post embarrassing pictures. It's cruel.

She's blocking the cyber bullies' emails and reporting them today!

We're having fun! We don't have time for cyber bullying!

**B** Work with a classmate. What do you think about cyber bullying?

*"I think cyber bullying is really cruel."*

## 3 Grammar 🔊 CD 2:17

**Simple present and present continuous**

| | |
|---|---|
| I **watch** the news every night. | I'm **watching** the news now. |
| You **study** on weekdays. | You're **studying** English now. |
| My dad **cooks** on Mondays. | He's **cooking** dinner now. |
| My friends and I **listen** to each other. | We're **listening** to a friend now. |
| They **donate** food to poor people. | They're **donating** food at the DIF now. |

**A** Complete the conversation with simple present or present continuous. Then check your answers with a classmate.

1. Julie _____works_____ (work) for the Red Cross.
   She _____is not working_____ (not / work) today.
2. He _____ (exercise) every day.
   He _____ (ride) his bike right now.
3. I _____ (text) my friends every day.
   I _____ (text) them right now.
4. Your friends usually _____ (walk) to school.
   Today they _____ (take) the bus.

**B** Work with a classmate. What do you usually do? What are you doing now?

**A:** What do you do on the weekends?   **B:** I ride my bike, and I watch TV.

## 4 Speaking  Breaking news

**A** Work with a classmate. Brainstorm news stories about social issues in the news now. Complete the chart.

| | News story 1 | News story 2 | News story 3 |
|---|---|---|---|
| **Person** | Workers | | |
| **Place** | Mexico City | | |
| **Actions** | Protesting, asking for justice | | |

**B** Work in a group. Perform the actions in your news stories. Your classmates guess the actions and the social issues. Take turns. Then listen to your classmates guessing actions. Evaluate them. Use the peer evaluation form on page 68.

**A:** There is a protest!   **B:** You are reporting the story!

▶ Can you talk about social issues?  ☐ Yes  ☐ No

# UNIT 9

## 5 Reading  Early morning

**A** Read the lyrics to the song. Check (✓) the pictures that match the lyrics. Then check your answers with a classmate.

It's early. No cars on the street.
He usually takes the bus, but not today.
He's walking. He's thinking.
He looks at his phone.
He's texting a friend.
No answer. It's early.

It's early. The house is quiet.
She usually gets up early, but not today.
She's sleeping. She's dreaming.
She's not looking at her phone.
She doesn't see the message.
She's sleeping. It's early.

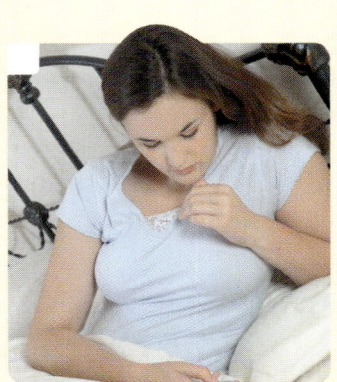

**B** Work with a classmate. What do you think is happening in the song?

"I think he is walking to school. He is thinking about the girl ..."

## 6 Listening  It's early. It's late.

**A** 🔊 CD 2:18  Listen to the song lyrics. Complete the sentences. Then check your answers with a classmate.

It's early. No cars on the street.
He usually _____ breakfast, but not today.
He's thinking. He _____ music.
He _____ his email.
He _____ his phone.
It's early.

It's late. The house is quiet.
She sometimes _____ TV, but not tonight.
She _____ a computer game.
She _____ news online.
She _____ with friends online.
It's late.

**B** Work with a classmate. Imagine this is a song. Create a rhythm. Practice your new song. Then present it to another group.

## 7 Writing  Our rap

Poverty       Protesting       Voting       Corruption

**A** Work in a small group. Research a social issue. Write a rap about it. Use simple present and present continuous.

> I'm not a cyber bully.
> You know that it's bad.
> I'm not a cyber bully.
> They make me sad!
>
> I'm not spreading rumors.
> I'm not hurting anyone
> I'm not a cyber bully.
> 'Cause it's just NO FUN!
>
> I'm ignoring cyber bullies.
> I don't hear what they say.
> I'm hanging out with my friends
> And having a great day!

**B** Exchange your rap with another group. Read your classmates' rap. Check that the forms of the simple present and the present continuous are correct.

## 8 Speaking  Rap it!

**A** Work with your group. Practice your rap.

**B** Present your rap to the class. Listen and evaluate classmates' songs. Use the peer evaluation form on page 68.

▶ Can you write and perform a rap about social issues?   ☐ Yes   ☐ No

# PEER EVALUATION — UNIT 9

## UNIT 9 page 65, exercise 4B  Speaking Breaking news

Listen to classmates guessing actions from news stories. Evaluate them. Write their scores.

**Score key**  3 = Great!  2 = Good  1 = Needs practice

| I am evaluating: | Grammar — uses the simple present and the present continuous correctly | Vocabulary — uses social issues words accurately | Fluency — speaks clearly and naturally | Total |
|---|---|---|---|---|
| 1. | | | | /9 |
| 2. | | | | /9 |
| 3. | | | | /9 |
| 4. | | | | /9 |
| 5. | | | | /9 |
| 6. | | | | /9 |

## UNIT 9 page 67, exercise 8B  Speaking Rap it!

Listen to your classmates presenting their raps. Evaluate them. Write their scores.

**Score key**  3 = Great!  2 = Good  1 = Needs practice

| I am evaluating: | Grammar — uses the simple present and the present continuous correctly | Vocabulary — uses social issues words accurately | Fluency — speaks clearly and naturally | Relevance — topic of rap is about a social issue | Total |
|---|---|---|---|---|---|
| 1. | | | | | /12 |
| 2. | | | | | /12 |
| 3. | | | | | /12 |
| 4. | | | | | /12 |
| 5. | | | | | /12 |
| 6. | | | | | /12 |

# SELF EVALUATION UNITS 7–9

Read the sentences. Write your score for each.

**Score key**
3 = I can do this very well  2 = I can do this  1 = I need more practice

| What I can do | Score |
|---|---|
| 1. I can ask for and tell the time.<br>*What's the time?*<br>*It's twenty to one.* | |
| 2. I can talk about jobs and work activities.<br>*Sandra is a flight attendant. She helps passengers.* | |
| 3. I can talk about activities people are doing right now.<br>*Chris isn't watching a movie. He's reading a book.* | |
| 4. I can describe online activities and daily routines.<br>*I'm checking email.*<br>*My friends are doing their homework.* | |
| 5. I can talk about social issues.<br>*We're talking about cyberbullying in our school.* | |
| 6. I can write and perform a rap about social issues.<br>*My rap:*<br>*I don't spread rumors.*<br>*I don't hurt anyone.*<br>*I'm not a cyber bully.* | |
| Total | |

# UNIT 7  Our day

**1** Write the times.

1. It's three o'clock in the afternoon.  It's 3:00 p.m.
2. It's twenty after ten in the morning.  _____
3. It's seven-oh-five in the evening.  _____
4. It's midnight.  _____
5. It's a quarter after five in the afternoon.  _____
6. It's a quarter to four in the morning.  It's 3:45 a.m.
7. It's half past two in the afternoon.  _____

**2** Look at Emilio's schedule. Then look at the underlined words in the sentences. Write the questions to the answers.

6:00 a.m.

7:45 a.m.

12:00 p.m.

3:30 p.m.

6:00 p.m.

8:00 p.m.

1. _What time does Emilio get up_ ?

   Emilio gets up <u>at six o'clock</u>.

2. _____?

   He does his homework <u>at half past three</u>.

3. _____?

   He <u>has lunch with his friends</u> at noon.

4. _____?

   He plays soccer <u>in the park</u> at 6 p.m.

5. _____?

   He <u>takes the bus to school</u> at a quarter to eight.

6. _____?

   He has dinner <u>with his family</u> at 8 p.m.

## UNIT 7 WORKBOOK

**3** Look at the information in parentheses. Complete the sentences with present continuous.

1. _I'm not studying_ math now. (I / not / study)
2. _____ a car. (He / fix)
3. _____ passengers on the airplane. (She / not / help)
4. _____ for our friends. (We / wait)
5. _____ to an emergency. (They / respond)
6. _____ patients. (I / not / see)

**4** Draw a mind map of the present continuous. Write the words below in the mind map. Then write an example for each one.

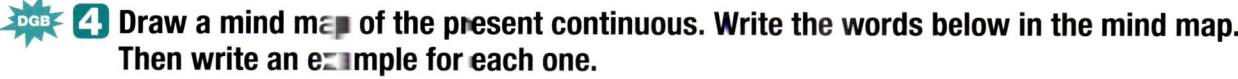

affirmative    negative    interrogative

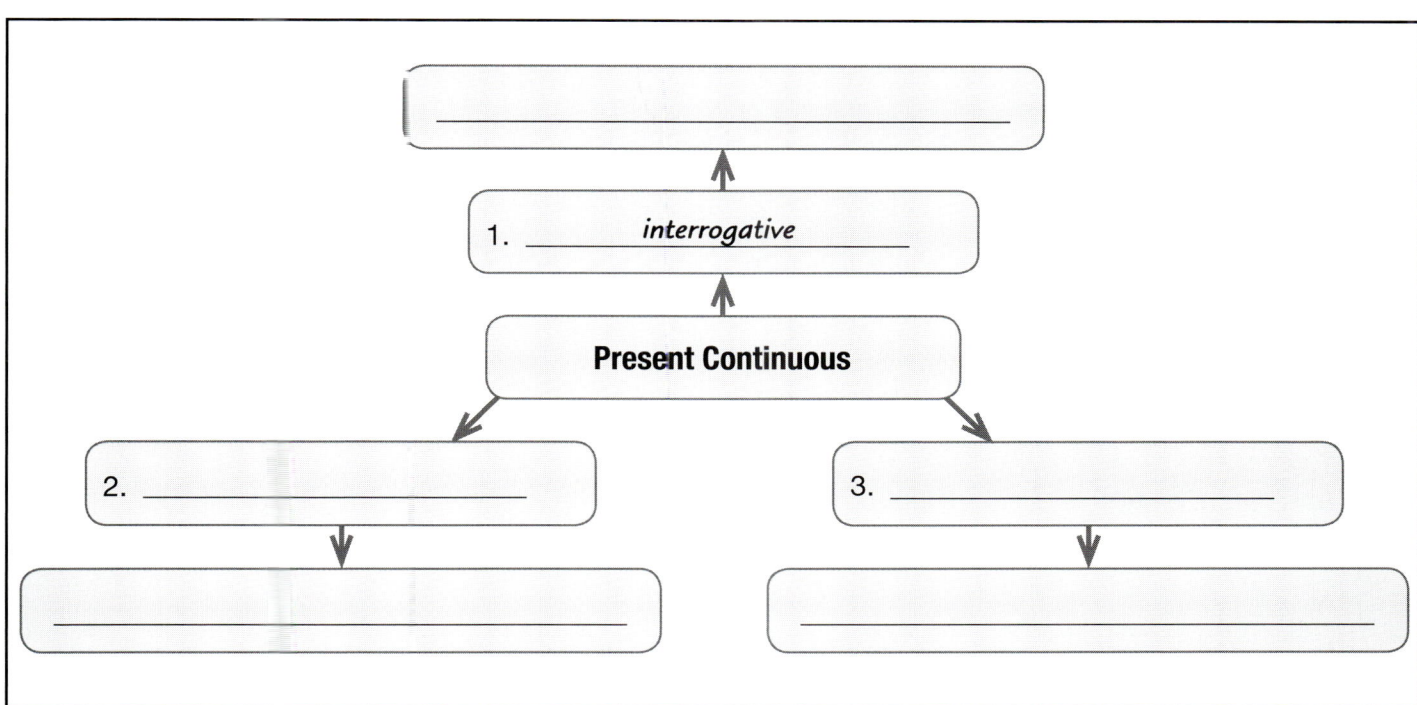

1. _interrogative_
2. _____
3. _____

Present Continuous

**5** Write five sentences about yourself, your family, or your friends in the present continuous. Use the affirmative and negative forms.

1. _My friends are sitting next to me_ .
2. _____ .
3. _____ .
4. _____ .
5. _____ .

# UNIT 8  What's happening?

**1** Put the letters in order to form colors.

1. klacb — *black*
2. yarg — _____
3. lerupp — _____
4. kinp — _____
5. owelly — _____
6. der — _____
7. granoe — _____
8. lueb — _____
9. neerg — _____
10. hitwe — _____

**2** Look at the chart. Complete the questions. Then write the answers.

|  | Clothing | Activities |
|---|---|---|
| Arturo | white shirt and blue pants | watch a movie |
| Tony | red sweater and black pants | read a book |
| Olivia and Emily | brown jackets and grey skirts | study for math test |
| Gloria | green dress | listen to music |
| Joe | orange shirt and black shorts | fix his car |
| Carlos and Sarah | yellow shirts and purple socks | sing a song |
| Ana | grey sweater and blue shorts | play the guitar |

1. **A:** *Is* Arturo *wearing* (wear) an orange shirt?
   **B:** No, he isn't. He's wearing a white shirt.

2. **A:** _____ Tony _____ (read) a book?
   **B:** _____.

3. **A:** _____ Olivia and Emily _____ (watch) a movie?
   **B:** _____.

4. **A:** _____ Gloria _____ (listen) to music?
   **B:** _____.

5. **A:** _____ Joe _____ (wear) purple shorts?
   **B:** _____.

6. **A:** _____ Carlos and Sarah _____ (sing) a song?
   **B:** _____.

7. **A:** _____ Ana _____ (play) the piano?
   **B:** _____.

# UNIT 8 WORKBOOK

**3** Use the information in parentheses to make questions.

1. (what / Hannah / do)            <u>What is Hannah doing</u>  ?
2. (where / Josh and Bill / chat)  _____ ?
3. (what / Ana / download)         _____ ?
4. (who / shop online)             _____ ?
5. (when / Gaby / check her email) _____ ?
6. (what / Raul / upload)          _____ ?
7. (what / Luis and Jorge / read)  _____ ?
8. (who / post a message)          _____ ?

**4** Look at the pictures. Then answer the questions from exercise 3.

Carlos

Luis and Jorge

Sofia

Raul

Josh and Bill

Hannah

Ana

Gaby

1. <u>Hannah's surfing the Internet</u>.
2. _____.
3. _____.
4. _____.
5. _____.
6. _____.
7. _____.
8. _____.

# UNIT 9 Our society

**1** Match the cyber bullying phrases to the sentences that describe them.

1. spreading rumors — _b_
2. making hurtful comments — ___
3. pretending to be someone else — ___
4. posting embarrassing pictures — ___
5. ignoring the bully — ___
6. collecting evidence — ___
7. reporting threats — ___
8. blocking emails — ___
9. spending time doing things you like — ___
10. sharing your feelings — ___

a. She's telling her parents.
b. They're saying things that aren't true.
c. He's creating an archive of the messages.
d. They're talking about how they feel.
e. He's saying mean things.
f. She's not answering the messages.
g. They're acting like they are other people.
h. I'm hanging out with my friends.
i. She's uploading humiliating images.
j. He's blocking their phone number

**2** Underline the errors. Rewrite the sentences. Use simple present or present continuous.

1. Sometimes I'm watching TV on the weekends.
   _Sometimes I watch TV on the weekends_.

2. He's report the threats now.
   _____.

3. I eating lunch now.
   _____.

4. My friends are usually texting me in the afternoon.
   _____.

5. She's no make hurtful comments online.
   _____!

6. They never acting like someone else.
   _____.

7. I'm often getting up at seven o'clock.
   _____.

8. What you do on the weekends?
   _____?

9. You go swimming on Tuesdays?
   _____?

10. Are your friends study now?
    _____?

UNIT 9 WORKBOOK

**3** Read the song lyrics. Complete the song. Use the actions below.

| hanging | chatting | watching | listening | sharing | talking | ~~playing~~ |

He's ___playing___ the guitar
He's _____ his feelings
And me? I'm _____ to a song
Just listening, listening, listening along.

He's _____ online
He's _____ on the phone
And me? I'm listening to a song
Just listening, listening, listening along.

He's _____ a movie
He's _____ out with a friend
And me? I'm listening to a song
Just listening, listening, listening along.

**4** Match the questions to the answers.

1. Who's checking email?  ___e___
2. When does Victor watch TV?  _____
3. What are they doing?  _____
4. What time is our English class?  _____
5. What are you studying now?  _____
6. Who do you eat lunch with?  _____
7. What are they downloading?  _____
8. What time do you get up?  _____
9. Why is she talking to the teacher?  _____
10. Where do you usually meet your friends?  _____

a. Because she's reporting a bully.
b. My friends.
c. At 6 a.m.
d. At the park.
e. She is.
f. Taking the bus to school.
g. In the evenings.
h. At 9 a.m. on Mondays and Wednesdays.
i. English.
j. Music.

**5** Describe what you are doing now and what you usually do on the weekends.

_____
_____
_____
_____
_____
_____

# SELF-CHECK   UNITS 7–9

## 1 The present continuous and simple present   ___/8
Fill in the blanks with the present continuous or simple present forms of the verbs.

At the moment, my friend, Sofia, _____ (exercise) in the park.
I _____ (not/exercise) today. I _____ (hang) out
with my friends Eduardo and Martha. They _____ (play) computer games,
and I _____ (listen) to music! I _____ (like) computer
games, but right now they _____ (play) so I _____ (wait).

## 2 Jobs   ___/7
Complete the sentences with the words below.

pilot   flight attendant   accountant   doctor   driver   electrician   police officer

1. He's waiting for passengers in his car. He's a _____.
2. She's flying the plane. She's the _____.
3. He's responding to an emergency. He's a _____.
4. She's helping passengers on the plane. She's a _____.
5. He's fixing electrical problems. He's an _____.
6. She's working with numbers. She's an _____.
7. He's seeing patients. He's a _____.

## 3 Wh- and yes/no questions and answers   ___/10
Match the questions to the correct responses.

1. What's Cecy wearing? ___
2. What time is it? ___
3. Is Sarah wearing a white T-shirt? ___
4. What's William doing? ___
5. Is he reporting threats to his teacher? ___
6. Who's wearing blue jeans? ___
7. Are you wearing my sweater? ___
8. When do you block email? ___
9. What are you doing right now? ___
10. What are David and Luis doing? ___

a. No, I'm not!
b. When I get cruel emails.
c. Yes, he is.
d. No, she isn't.
e. They're eating dinner.
f. He's exercising.
g. Enrique.
h. It's ten thirty.
i. I'm reading.
j. A pink skirt.

## Score
Count total points.

Total score: ___/25

**25–23 points** Great!   **22–20 points** Good   **19–17 points** Needs practice   **Below 17 points** Ask for help!

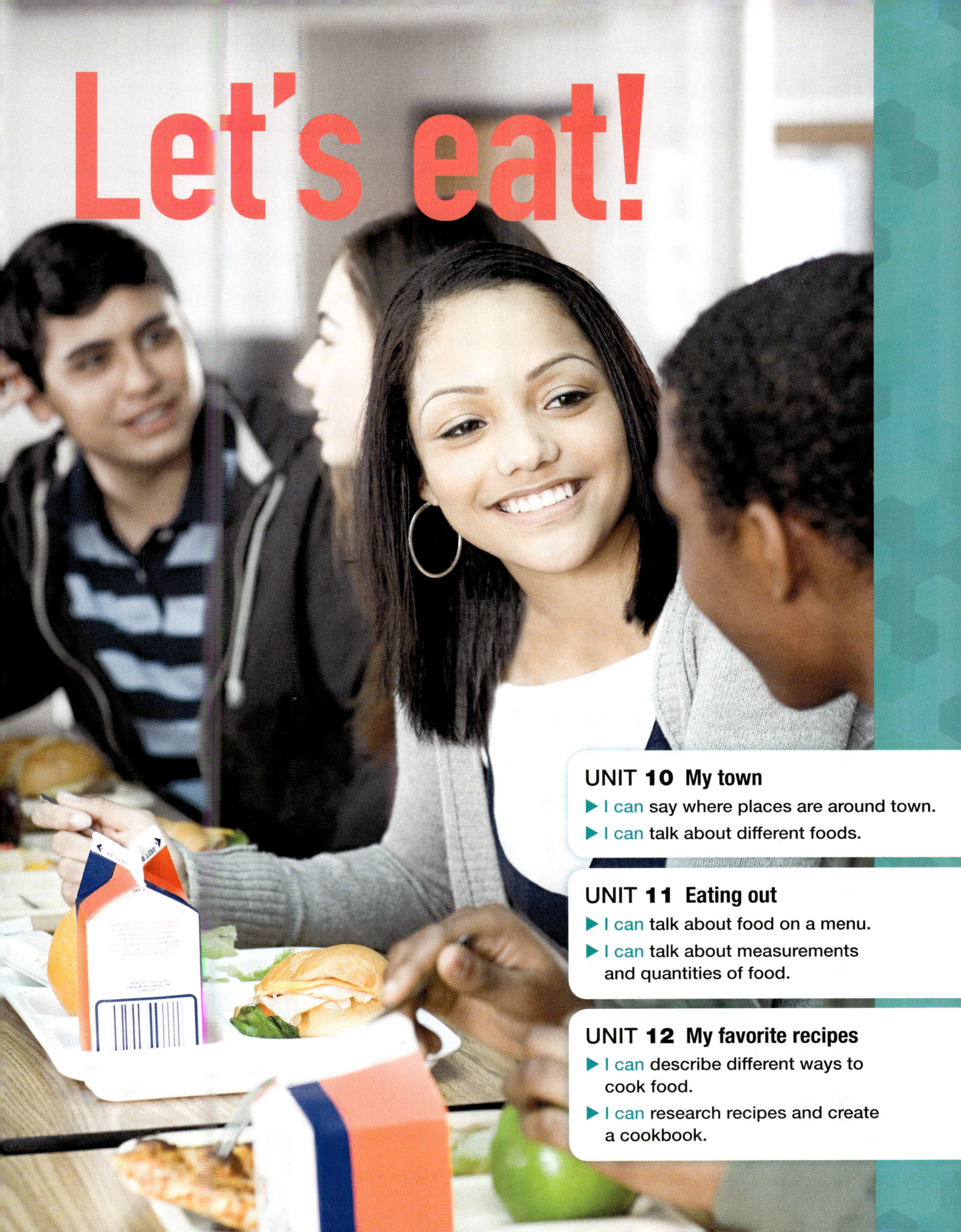

# Let's eat!

### UNIT 10 My town
▶ I can say where places are around town.
▶ I can talk about different foods.

### UNIT 11 Eating out
▶ I can talk about food on a menu.
▶ I can talk about measurements and quantities of food.

### UNIT 12 My favorite recipes
▶ I can describe different ways to cook food.
▶ I can research recipes and create a cookbook.

# UNIT 10  My town

## 1 Vocabulary  Places around town

**A** 🔊 CD 2:19  Listen and repeat.

bank    bookstore    bus stop    coffee shop

gas station    hotel    newsstand    supermarket

**B** Work with a classmate. Point to pictures in exercise A. Ask and answer questions about the places around town. Take turns.

**A:** *What's the place in this picture?*
**B:** *It's a bank.*

## 2 Language in context  There's a coffee shop.

**A** 🔊 CD 2:20  Listen to people talk about their town. Circle what they like and underline the places they go.

**Lety:** I like (computer games). There is an <u>internet café</u> on Calle Hidalgo. I play computer games there.

**Martin:** I like books. There is a bookstore across from the bank. I buy books there.

**Susan:** I like coffee. There is a coffee shop next to the park. I have coffee and meet my friends there.

**B** Work with a classmate. How often do you go to the places in exercise 1A?

**A:** *I go to the bus stop every day.*
**B:** *My mom goes to the bank once a week.*

# UNIT 10

## 3 Grammar  CD 2:21
**There is** and **there are**; prepositions of location

There's = There is
**There's** a bank on Clark Street.

| | |
|---|---|
| **There is** a **b**ank **on** Clark Street. | **There are** two newsstands **in** the park. |
| **There is** a **b**ookstore **next to** the bank. | **There are** two hotels **across from** the park. |
| **There is** a **c**offee shop **between** the bookstore and the park. | |

**A** Circle the correct words. Then check your answers with a classmate.

1. There **(is)** / **are** a bank across from the newsstand.
2. There **are** / **is** two supermarkets in my town.
3. There is a gas station **between** / **in** the bank and the bookstore.
4. There **are** / **is** a park next to our school.
5. There are two hotels **next to** / **between** the park.
6. There **is** / **are** five bus stops on Calle Madero.

**B** Work with a classmate. Talk about where places are in your town.

"There's a park next to the school."

## 4 Speaking  A town map

**A** Work in a small group. Make a list of places and write where they are. Draw a town map.

| Place | Location |
|---|---|
| bank | next to the supermarket |

**B** Present your town map to another group. Use the prepositions of location from exercise 3.

"There's a bank next to the supermarket."

▶ Can you say where places are around town?  ☐ Yes  ☐ No

UNIT 10

## 5 Vocabulary  Food

**A** 🔊 CD 2:22  Write the words under the pictures. Then listen and check your answers.

| ~~cheese~~ | fish | apples | milk | ~~eggs~~ | rice |
| beef / steak | pasta | strawberries | potatoes | ~~chicken~~ | tomatoes |

**Dairy**

_cheese_  _____

**Fruit**

_____  _____

**Grains**

_____  _____

**Vegetables**

_____  _____

**Meat and protein**

_____  _eggs_  _____  _chicken_

**B** Work with a classmate. Ask and answer questions about the food in the pictures. Take turns.

**A:** Do you like grains?
**B:** No, I don't. I prefer fruit.
**A:** What's your favorite fruit?
**B:** I like apples.

## 6 Conversation  *There are strawberries and apples.*

**A** 🔊 CD 2:23  Listen.

**Oliver:** What do you want for breakfast?
**Amelia:** I don't know. What's in the refrigerator?
**Oliver:** There's milk and fruit. There are eggs, too.
**Amelia:** What fruit do we have?
**Oliver:** There are strawberries and apples.
**Amelia:** Ok — I want cereal with milk and strawberries.
**Oliver:** Hmm … That sounds good. But I want eggs, too!

**B** Practice the conversation with a classmate.

80

## 7 Grammar 🔊 CD 2:24

**Count and noncount nouns**

| Count nouns | | Spelling: plurals | |
|---|---|---|---|
| an egg | two eggs | apple | → apples |
| a potato | three potatoes | tomato | → tomatoes |
| | | strawberry | → strawberries |
| **Noncount nouns** | | | |
| milk    cheese    beef | | | |

**A** Write the words in the correct columns. Then check your answers with a classmate.

| rice | cheese | tomato | steak | strawberry | fish | potato |
| egg | milk | apple | chicken | cereal | beef | |

| Count nouns | | Noncount nouns | |
|---|---|---|---|
| _egg_ | _____ | _beef_ | _____ |
| _____ | _____ | _____ | _____ |
| _____ | _____ | _____ | |
| | | _____ | |

**B** Work with a classmate. What's in your refrigerator?

**A:** What's in your refrigerator?
**B:** There's milk and there are tomatoes.

## 8 Pronunciation /s/ and /z/ sounds

**A** 🔊 CD 2:25 Listen and repeat. Notice that some words have an /s/ sound and others have a /z/ sound in the plural form.

| /s/ sound | /z/ sound |
|---|---|
| books  carrots  students  shirts | apples  teachers  strawberries  chairs |

**B** 🔊 CD 2:26 Listen. Circle the words that have an /s/ sound and underline the words that have a /z/ sound. Then check your answers with a classmate.

(desks)   coats   pencils   papers   socks   tomatoes   banks   eggs

▶ Can you talk about different foods?  ☐ Yes  ☐ No

# UNIT 11 Eating out

## 1 Vocabulary  On the menu

**A** CD 2:27 Write the words under the pictures. Then listen and check your answers.

| soup | hot dogs | spaghetti | ~~ice cream~~ | salad | hamburger | sandwich | pizza |

1. _ice cream_   2. _____   3. _____   4. _____

5. _____   6. _____   7. _____   8. _____

**B** Work with a classmate. Make a picture dictionary with the food words you know. Then present your dictionary to two other classmates.

## 2 Language in context  Is there spaghetti today?

**A** CD 2:28 Listen to a conversation between Martha and a waiter. Underline the food. Then check your answers with a classmate.

> **Martha:** Is there <u>spaghetti</u> today?
> **Waiter:** No, I'm sorry. There isn't. Do you want some salad?
> **Martha:** Um … no, thanks. Are there any hamburgers?
> **Waiter:** No, there aren't. There is some soup!
> **Martha:** Er … no thanks. What about hot dogs?
> **Waiter:** Yes! There are a few hot dogs.
> **Martha:** Great. I want two hot dogs, please!

**B** Work with a classmate. What do you like to eat in restaurants?

"I like tacos and salad."

82

## 3 Grammar 🔊 CD 2:29

**Is there …? / Are there …?; some, any**

| | |
|---|---|
| **Is there any** pizza? | There's **some** salad. |
| Yes, **there is**. / No, **there isn't**. | There are **some** hamburgers. |
| **Are there any** sandwiches? | There isn't **any** cheese. |
| Yes, **there are**. / No, **there aren't**. | There aren't **any** hot dogs. |

### A Circle the correct words.

1. **(Is)** / **Are** there any milk? Yes, there is **(some)** / **any** milk in the refrigerator.
2. There **are** **some** / **any** hot dogs, but there aren't **any** / **some** sandwiches.
3. **Are** / **Is** there **any** / **some** yogurt? Yes, there is.
4. There **is** / **are** some sandwiches, but there isn't **some** / **any** pizza.
5. There **is** **some** / **any** cheese, but there **isn't** / **aren't** any hamburgers.

### B Work with a classmate. Ask and answer questions. Take turns.

| | | | | |
|---|---|---|---|---|
| tomatoes | ✓ | rice | ✗ |
| cheese | ✗ | meat | ✗ |
| bread | ✓ | strawberries | ✓ |
| apples | ✗ | pasta | ✓ |

**A:** Are there any tomatoes?
**B:** Yes, there are some tomatoes.

## 4 Speaking  My grocery list

### A Complete the grocery list with food your family usually buys. Then go to page 94 and complete the chart.

| | |
|---|---|
| **Dairy** | milk, |
| **Fruit** | apples, |
| **Vegetables** | carrots, |
| **Grains** | corn tortillas, |
| **Protein** | chicken, |

### B Work in a small group. Choose a list and present it. Listen to your classmates' presentations. Use the peer evaluation form on page 90.

"We usually buy a lot of tomatoes and some cheese."

▶ Can you talk about food on a menu?  ☐ Yes  ☐ No

UNIT 11

83

# UNIT 11

## 5 Vocabulary  Measurements and quantities

**A** 🔊 CD 2:30  Complete the phrases with the words below. Then listen and check your answers.

**Measuring food**

> teaspoon   liter   ~~stick~~   grams   ~~tablespoon~~   cup   kilo   ~~pinch~~

1. a _tablespoon_ of milk
2. a _____ of sugar
3. a _____ of flour
4. a _pinch_ of salt
5. a _____ of fish
6. 100 _____ of cheese
7. half a _____ of water
8. a _stick_ of butter

**B** Work with a classmate. Look at the pictures in exercise A. Ask and answer questions. Take turns.

**A:** What's in picture 1?
**B:** It's a tablespoon of milk.

## 6 Conversation  We need a kilo of chicken.

**A** 🔊 CD 2:31  Listen.

> **Victor:** Let's make chicken and rice for lunch today.
> **Gabriela:** Good idea! How much chicken and rice do we need?
> **Victor:** Let's look at the recipe. We need a kilo of chicken and 300 grams of rice.
> **Gabriela:** Oh no! There isn't any rice.
> **Victor:** Is there any chicken?
> **Gabriela:** Yes, there's a little chicken.
> **Victor:** Are there any tortillas?
> **Gabriela:** Yes, there are a few tortillas.
> **Victor:** How about chicken tacos?
> **Gabriela:** That sounds good!

**B** Practice the conversation with a classmate.

## 7 Grammar 🔊 CD 2:32

**How much …? / How many …?; a lot of, some, a little, a few, much, many, any**

| How much + noncount nouns | | | How many + count nouns | | |
|---|---|---|---|---|---|
| How **much** milk is there? | | | How **many** apples do you need? | | |
| There is | a lot of / some / a little | milk. | I need | a lot of / some / a few | apples. |
| There isn't | much / any | milk. | I don't need | many / any | apples. |

**A** Complete the following questions and statements. Use the clues in parentheses. Then check your answers with a classmate.

1. How ___much___ cheese is there?
2. There are _____ strawberries. (three)
3. How _____ hot dogs are there?
4. There is _____ yogurt. (a teaspoon)
5. We don't need _____ eggs.

**B** Work with a classmate. Create questions or answers for exercise A. Take turns.

**A:** How much cheese is there?
**B:** There's a little cheese.

## 8 Speaking  My favorite food

**A** Write your favorite foods in the chart and say how much / how many you eat of each food in one week.

| Me | How much / many a week? | Name: _____ | How much / many a week? |
|---|---|---|---|
| hamburgers | three | | |

**B** Work with a classmate. Ask questions using *how much* or *how many*. Answer questions using *a lot of*, *some*, *a few*, *a little*, or *any*. Take turns.

**A:** How many hamburgers do you eat in a week?
**B:** I eat a lot of hamburgers! I eat three a week.

▶ Can you talk about measurements and quantities of food?
☐ Yes  ☐ No

# UNIT 12 My favorite recipes

## 1 Vocabulary  Cooking verbs

**A** 🔊 CD 2:33  Listen and repeat.

**chop** carrots   **mix** water and flour   **fry** potatoes   **boil** eggs

**measure** flour   **roast** chicken   **bake** a cake   **melt** cheese

**B** Work with a classmate. Talk about the actions you know how to do.

"I know how to chop carrots."

## 2 Language in context  How much are strawberries?

**A** 🔊 CD 2:34  Listen to a conversation in a shop. Underline the food you hear. Circle the quantities. Then check your answers with a classmate.

| | |
|---|---|
| **Penelope:** | Good morning! I want to bake a cake today! Do you have any flour? |
| **Shopkeeper:** | Yes, I do. How much do you want? |
| **Penelope:** | 500 grams, please, and I need one kilo of eggs, too. |
| **Shopkeeper:** | Ok. Do you need some milk? |
| **Penelope:** | Yes, one liter, please. Oh! How much are strawberries? |
| **Shopkeeper:** | One kilo is $20 pesos. |
| **Penelope:** | Ok—half a kilo please. That's all I need. How much is that? |
| **Shopkeeper:** | Nothing! Please bring me some of your cake! |

**B** Work with a classmate. What food does your family like to cook?

"We eat quesadillas every day."

## 3 Grammar  CD 2:35

**How much / is /are …?; Numbers 20–101**

**How much is** the pizza?
It's $120 pesos.

**How much is** the chicken?
It's $60 pesos a kilo.

**How much are** the strawberries?
They're $20 pesos a kilo.

**How much are** the hamburgers?
They're $45 pesos each.

**Numbers 20–101**

| | |
|---|---|
| 20 twenty | 60 sixty |
| 30 thirty | 70 seventy |
| 40 forty | 80 eighty |
| 50 fifty | 90 ninety |

100 a hundred
101 one hundred and one

**A** Write *is* or *are* to complete the questions. Then check your answers with a classmate.

1. How much ___is___ spaghetti?
2. How much _____ hamburgers?
3. How much _____ ice cream?
4. How much _____ hot dogs?
5. How much _____ fish?

**B** Work with a classmate. Ask the questions in exercise A. Guess the answers. Take turns.

**A:** How much is spaghetti in a restaurant?
**B:** It's usually $70 pesos.

## 4 Speaking  Our lunch plans

**A** Work with a classmate. Choose one of the situations. Create a role play.

Sharing a recipe

Ordering food over the phone

Grocery shopping

**A:** Do you know how to make rice?
**B:** Yes, I do. You boil two cups of water. Then …

**B** Work in a group. Present your role play to your classmates.

▶ Can you describe different ways to cook food?   ☐ Yes   ☐ No

UNIT 12

## 5 Reading  English Sunday dinner

**A** Read about some traditional food from England. What is it? Check your answer with a classmate.

> My name is Sarah. I'm from a town called Oxford, in England. Many English people eat Sunday dinner with their families. We usually make beef or chicken with potatoes and vegetables.
>
> Today I'm making chicken with potatoes. I usually buy one chicken and a lot of potatoes. My family loves potatoes! I roast the chicken. I boil the potatoes, then I roast them, too. It's not expensive to make. It's about £20 for five people.
>
> Sometimes people go to a restaurant for Sunday dinner. There's a good restaurant in Oxford, but the Sunday dinner there is £20 per person! We prefer to cook at home.

**B** Answer the questions. Circle T (true) or F (false).

1. To make Sunday dinner, you fry chicken.　　T　(F)
2. Sarah's family loves potatoes.　　T　F
3. Sunday dinner is very expensive to make.　　T　F
4. Sarah often eats meat on Sundays.　　T　F
5. People never go to a restaurant for Sunday dinner.　　T　F

## 6 Listening  Italian food

**A** 🔊 CD 2:36  Listen to an Italian chef talking about a traditional recipe. What food is it? Check your answer with a classmate.

**B** 🔊 CD 2:37  Listen again. Answer the questions. Then check your answers with a classmate.

1. What ingredients are in the recipe? _salt, tomatoes, onions, cheese, beef_
2. How much beef does he need? _____
3. How does he cook the tomatoes and onions? _____
4. Is there any fruit in the recipe? _____
5. How does the chef cook the spaghetti? _____

UNIT 12

## 7 Writing  Our cookbook

**A** Work in a group. Research different recipes. Make a list of the recipes for your cookbook.

| a recipe from your community | a recipe from your region | a recipe from Mexico | a recipe from another country |
|---|---|---|---|
|  |  | |  |
| Enchiladas Potosinas | Zacahuil | Chiles en Nogada | Ajiaco |

**B** Write your cookbook. Use food vocabulary and cooking verbs. Follow the chart.

1. Choose a cover.
2. Write an introduction.
3. Write the recipe from your community.
4. Write the recipe from your region.
5. Write the recipe from Mexico.
6. Write the recipe from another country.

## 8 Speaking  Class cookbooks

**A** Work with your group. Practice your cookbook presentation.

*My recipe is for Pozole. First, you ...*

**B** Present your cookbook to another group. Then decide how you want to share your cookbook.

▶ Can you research recipes and create a cookbook?   ☐ Yes   ☐ No

# PEER EVALUATION UNIT 11

**UNIT 11** page 94, exercise 1

Listen to your classmates present their inventories. Evaluate them. Write their scores.

**Score key**
3 = Great!  2 = Good  1 = Needs practice

| I am evaluating: | Vocabulary | | | Total |
| --- | --- | --- | --- | --- |
| | classifies food he/she has at home accurately | classifies classroom objects accurately | classifies spoken languages in Mexico accurately | |
| 1. | | | | /9 |
| 2. | | | | /9 |
| 3. | | | | /9 |
| 4. | | | | /9 |
| 5. | | | | /9 |
| 6. | | | | /9 |

# SELF EVALUATION  UNITS 10–12

Read the sentences. Write your score for each.

**Score key**
3 = I can do this very well   2 = I can do this   1 = I need more practice

| What I can do | Score |
|---|---|
| 1. I can say where places are around town.<br>There are two bus stops on my street.<br>There's a bank between the hotel and the supermarket. | |
| 2. I can talk about different foods.<br>There's fish and steak in my refrigerator.<br>Do you like fish? | |
| 3. I can talk about food on a menu.<br>Is there pizza today?<br>I want two hot dogs, please. | |
| 4. I can talk about measurements and quantities of food.<br>There are a few strawberries.<br>I need a liter of milk. | |
| 5. I can describe different ways to cook food.<br>You boil some water. Then you add the rice. | |
| 6. I can research recipes and create a cookbook.<br>This is a recipe from my town. You need chicken, rice, and vegetables. | |
| Total | |

# UNIT 10  Places around town

**1** Complete the crossword with places vocabulary.

Across →
3. We buy magazines at the _____.
6. She meets her friends at the _____ on the weekends.
8. They buy food at the _____.

Down ↓
1. Tourists often sleep in a _____.
2. He goes to the _____ for gas.
4. He waits for a bus at the _____.
5. I buy books at the _____.
7. They put their money in a _____.

**2** Look at the picture. Complete the sentences with the words below.

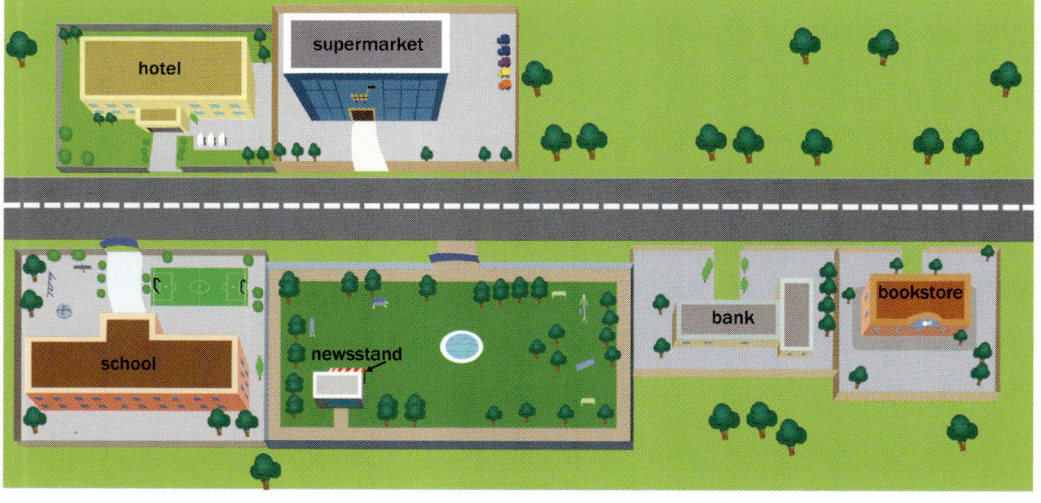

~~on~~

next to

between

across from

in

1. There's a school ____on____ Calle Hidalgo.
2. There's a bank _____ the bookstore and the park.
3. There's a newsstand _____ the park.
4. There's a hotel _____ the school.
5. There's a supermarket _____ the hotel.

# UNIT 10 WORKBOOK

**3** Circle the correct words to complete the sentences.

1. An egg is a form of _____.
   a. dairy            b. vegetables            **(c. protein)**
2. Rice is a _____.
   a. fruit            b. grain                 c. meat
3. A potato is a _____.
   a. protein          b. grain                 c. vegetable
4. Cheese is _____.
   a. grain            b. dairy                 c. fruit
5. A strawberry is _____.
   a. fruit            b. grains                c. vegetables
6. Beef is _____.
   a. dairy            b. protein               c. fruit

**4** Write the plural form of the words.

1. apple _____apples_____
2. strawberry _____
3. park _____
4. family _____
5. tomato _____
6. banana _____
7. bookstore _____
8. nationality _____
9. supermarket _____
10. potato _____
11. country _____
12. egg _____
13. bank _____
14. café _____
15. emergency _____
16. vegetable _____

**5** Circle the words to complete the sentences.

1. There **(is)** / are an apple on the table.
2. There **is** / are milk in the refrigerator.
3. There is / **are** tomatoes at the market.
4. There **is** / are beef in hamburgers.
5. There **is** / are rice in that recipe.
6. There is / **are** gas stations in my city.
7. There is / **are** hotels in my town.
8. There **is** / are cheese on the table.
9. There is / **are** eggs in the refrigerator.
10. There **is** / are yogurt in my smoothie.
11. There is / **are** strawberries at the store.
12. There **is** / are fish at the supermarket.

# UNIT 11  Eating out

**1** Choose one of the topics below. Circle it. Make an inventory of words for it. Then listen to your classmates' inventories. Evaluate the presentations. Use the peer evaluation form on page 90.

classroom objects                                          languages in Mexico

_____                    _____
_____                    _____
_____                    _____
_____                    _____
_____                    _____
_____                    _____
_____                    _____
_____                    _____
_____                    _____

**2** Complete the questions with the correct form of *there is / there are*. Answer the questions with the correct form of *there is / there are*, *some*, and *any*.

1. **A:** _Is there_ _____ any ice cream?
   **B:** Yes, _there's some_ _____ ice cream.

2. **A:** _____ any salad?
   **B:** No, _____ salad.

3. **A:** _____ any hot dogs?
   **B:** No, _____ hot dogs.

4. **A:** _____ any pizza?
   **B:** Yes, _____ pizza.

5. **A:** _____ any soup?
   **B:** No, _____ soup.

6. **A:** _____ any sandwiches?
   **B:** Yes, _____ sandwiches.

7. **A:** _____ any spaghetti?
   **B:** Yes, _____ spaghetti.

8. **A:** _____ any hamburgers?
   **B:** No, _____ hamburgers.

# UNIT 11 WORKBOOK

**3** Put the letters in order to make measurements and quantities.

1. o k l i     _____kilo_____
2. p o t s a n e o     _____
3. t r e i l     _____
4. c h i n p     _____
5. t i c k s     _____
2. p u c     _____
3. m a g s r     _____
4. s n o p e b o t a l     _____

**4** Complete the sentences with words from exercise 3.

1. There's a ____liter____ of milk in the refrigerator.
2. We need 400 _____ of beef.
3. He is putting a _____ of salt on his eggs.
4. She always has a _____ of sugar in her coffee.
5. They need a _____ of butter to make the cake.
6. Do you want a _____ of tea?
7. We buy a _____ of bananas every week.
8. She is putting a _____ of sugar in her tea. That's a lot! I only put a teaspoon in my tea.

**5** Complete the conversations. Use the correct form of *there is*, *there are*, and *how much*, *how many*, *a little*, *any*, and *a few*.

1. **Juan:** ___Are there___ any apples?
   **Lety:** Yes, _____. _____ do you want?
   **Juan:** I want _____ apples, please.

2. **Manuel:** Oh no! We don't have _____ cheese!
   **Alicia:** _____ cheese do we need?
   **Manuel:** Just _____.

3. **Emma:** I'm hungry! What's for breakfast?
   **Susan:** Well, _____ cereal, and _____ bananas.
   **Emma:** Great! I want bananas on my cereal. _____ _____ milk?
   **Susan:** Yes, _____ _____ milk.

4. **Lauren:** I'm making strawberry ice cream.
   **Jorge:** _____ strawberries do you need?
   **Lauren:** I need half a kilo of strawberries. I also need a cup of sugar, two eggs and a cup of milk.
   **Jorge:** Uh oh. _____ _____ sugar, and _____ only _____ strawberries.
   **Lauren:** Oh no!

95

# UNIT 12  My favorite recipes

**1** Complete the clues with cooking verbs. Then complete the crossword.

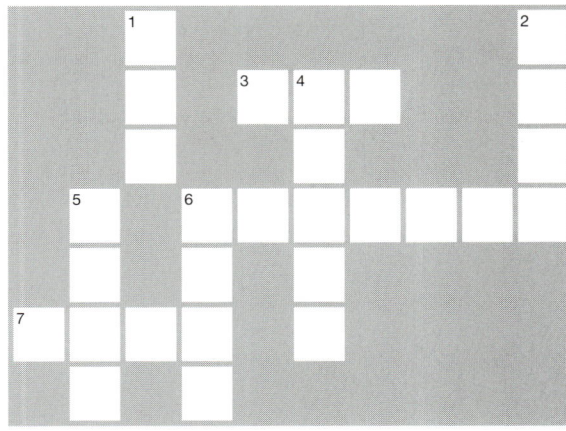

Across →
3. _____ potatoes
6. _____ flour
7. _____ an egg in water

Down ↓
1. _____ flour, milk, and eggs
2. _____ a cake
4. _____ beef
5. _____ vegetables
6. _____ cheese on a hamburger

**2** Complete the conversation. Use some of the words from exercise 1.

**Lucia:** What are you doing?
**Cesar:** I'm making a cake for a friend. She's sick.
**Lucia** That's nice! I like to _____ cakes, too. Do you want my help?
                                              1
**Cesar:** Yes! Please _____ two cups of flour, and _____ a stick of butter.
                       2                                    3
**Lucia:** OK. What else?
**Cesar:** Do you want to _____ the flour, sugar, and eggs together?
                           4
**Lucia:** Sure. No problem.

**3** Circle the correct word to complete each sentence.

1. How much _____ the fish?
   a. have                b. is                  c. are
2. How _____ is the chicken?
   a. many               b. much                c. a few
3. How much _____ the carrots?
   a. have               b. is                  c. are
4. How many _____ do you want?
   a. hot dogs          b. yogurt              c. cheese
5. I want _____ rice.
   a. few                b. much                c. a little
6. I eat _____ cheese every day.
   a. some               b. a few               c. many

# UNIT 12 WORKBOOK

**4** Read about a traditional recipe from Switzerland. Check the correct responses.

Switzerland is a country next to Italy and France. In Switzerland, people eat a traditional dish. It's *fondue*! People eat fondue in a restaurant or at home with their families. You melt cheese and eat it. It's fun to eat. Sometimes people boil potatoes and make a salad. Then they eat the potatoes and salad with the fondue. It's expensive to make fondue. You need a kilo of fondue for about four people. It costs about 25 euros in a restaurant!

1. What is the traditional dish?
   - [ ] Potatoes and salad
   - [ ] Fondue

2. Where do people eat fondue?
   - [ ] Italy
   - [ ] Switzerland

3. Where's Switzerland?
   - [ ] Next to Italy
   - [ ] Between Italy and France

4. What's in the recipe?
   - [ ] Cheese
   - [ ] Fruit

5. How do people cook the potatoes?
   - [ ] They fry the potatoes.
   - [ ] They boil the potatoes.

6. How much cheese do four people eat?
   - [ ] A little
   - [ ] A kilo

**5** Match the questions to the answers.

1. How much is the chicken?  __b__
2. Where do you go for gas?  ____
3. How much milk do we have?  ____
4. How much ice do we have?  ____
5. Where is the bank?  ____
6. Do you like cake?  ____
7. How do you go to school?  ____
8. Do you eat fondue?  ____

a. We have 1 kilo.
b. It's $60 pesos a kilo.
c. It's on Calle Hidalgo.
d. Yes, I do.
e. No. I don't like cheese.
f. I take the bus.
g. I go to a gas station next to the store.
h. We have 2 liters.

# SELF-CHECK  UNITS 10–12

## 1 My town  /7
Look at the picture. Read the sentences. Circle T (true) or F (false).

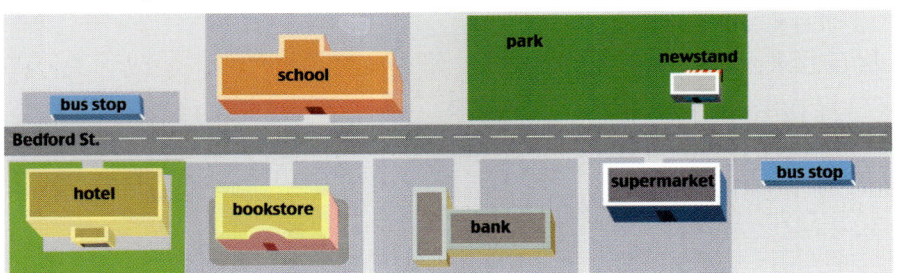

1. There's a park next to the newsstand.  T  F
2. The newsstand is in the park.  T  F
3. There's a bookstore across from the school.  T  F
4. There are three bus stops are on Bedford Street.  T  F
5. The bookstore is between the hotel and the bank.  T  F
6. The supermarket is across from the bank.  T  F
7. There's a gas station next to the supermarket.  T  F

## 2 There is / there are  /6
Complete the questions and sentences with the correct form of *there is / there are*.

1. _____ any tacos.
2. _____ any cheese?
3. _____ some cake.
4. Yes, _____ a lot of hamburgers.
5. _____ any strawberries?
6. _____ any salad.

## 3 How much / How many / a few / a little / any  /12
Complete the answers with *a little* or *a few*. Then write the questions.

1. **A:** How _____?
   **B:** There's _____ milk.

2. **A:** How _____?
   **B:** There are _____ apples.

3. **A:** How _____?
   **B:** There's _____ pasta.

4. **A:** Are _____?
   **B:** Yes, there are _____ tomatoes.

5. **A:** Is there _____?
   **B:** Yes, there is _____ water.

6. **A:** Is _____?
   **B:** No, there isn't _____ salad.

## Score
Count total points.

Total score: ___ /25

**25–23 points** Great!  **22–20 points** Good  **19–17 points** Needs practice  **Below 17 points** Ask for help!

**LEVEL 1 PROJECT**

# LEVEL 1 Our Mexico!

## 1 Preparation

**A** Work in a group of three or four students. Talk about the people, activities, places, geographical features, and foods that represent *your* Mexico. Then complete the chart.

| People | Activities | Places | Geographical features | Food |
|---|---|---|---|---|
| my family | folk dances | the plaza | mountains | chiles en nogada |

**B** Work in your group. Talk about what you want to put on your poster.

**A:** *I want pictures of places in our town.*
**B:** *Great idea! I think pictures or drawings of activities we like are good, too.*

**C** Work in your group. Decide what each person will do for the poster presentation, and when you will meet. Write the information in the chart.

| Name | Responsible for ... |
|---|---|
| | |

Meeting day and time

## 2 Poster presentation

**A** Work in your group. Decide who will present each topic. Practice your presentation.

**A:** *"Ok. I can talk about ... What do you want to present?"*

**B** Present your information. Listen to classmates' presentations. Evaluate them. Use the peer evaluation form on page 100.

99

# PEER EVALUATION — LEVEL 1 project

**LEVEL 1** page 99, exercise 2B

Listen to your classmates talking about their poster presentations. Evaluate the presentations. Write their scores.

**Score key**
3 = Great!   2 = Good   1 = Needs practice

| I am evaluating: | Grammar<br>uses the simple present correctly | Vocabulary<br>uses people, places, activities, geographical features, and food words accurately | Fluency<br>speaks clearly and naturally | Total |
|---|---|---|---|---|
| 1. | | | | /9 |
| 2. | | | | /9 |
| 3. | | | | /9 |
| 4. | | | | /9 |
| 5. | | | | /9 |
| 6. | | | | /9 |

# SELF EVALUATION — LEVEL 1

Read the sentences. Write your score for each.

**Score key**
3 = I can do this very well   2 = I can do this   1 = I need more practice

| What I can do | Score |
|---|---|
| 1. I can talk about myself and my family.<br>My family lives in Guadalajara.<br>I have two brothers and a sister.<br>We hang out with our cousins on the weekends. | |
| 2. I can talk about community activities in my region.<br>Many people walk in Bosque Los Colomos park.<br>Teenagers hang out with their friends. | |
| 3. I can describe geographical features in my region.<br>There are mountains, waterfalls and beaches in my region. | |
| 4. I can describe traditional Mexican food and how to make it.<br>We often eat enchiladas con mole in Mexico. I make them with chicken, chocolate, chiles, and tortillas. | |
| 5. I can give a poster presentation.<br>This is a picture of Mexico. There are a lot of mountains in our region. These mountains are the Sierra Madre. | |
| Total | |

# English/Spanish dictionary

| English | Spanish |
|---|---|
| a | un(a) |
| a.m. | a.m. |
| a few | unos pocos |
| a little | un poco |
| a lot | mucho / bastante |
| a quarter to | quarto para |
| a quarter after | quince después |
| about | acerca |
| accountant | contador |
| across from | al otro lado de / del otro lado |
| act (v) | actuar |
| action | acción |
| activity | actividad |
| address | dirección |
| adjective | adjetivo |
| adult | adulto |
| adverb | adverbio |
| affirmative | afirmativo(a) |
| after | después |
| afternoon | tarde (después de mediodía) |
| age | edad |
| airplane | avión / aeronave |
| airport | aeropuerto |
| along | a lo largo de / conmigo |
| all | todo(a) |
| also | también |
| always | siempre |
| an | un(a) |
| and | y |
| another | otro / uno más |
| answer (n) | respuesta |
| answer (v) | responder |
| any | algún |
| anyone | alguno(a) |
| appearance | apariencia |
| apple | manzana |
| application | aplicación |
| apply | aplicar / usar |
| archeological | arqueológico |
| archive (n) | archivo |
| area | área |
| around | alrededor |
| article | artículo |
| artwork | obra de arte |
| ask | preguntar |
| at | en |

| English | Spanish |
|---|---|
| Atlantic Ocean | Océano Atlántico |
| aunt | tía |
| Australia | Australia |
| Australian | australiano(a) |
| average | promedio |
| bad | malo(a) |
| bake | hornear |
| bald | calvo |
| banana | plátano |
| bank (n) | banco |
| baseball | béisbol |
| basketball | basketbol |
| be | ser / estar |
| beach | playa |
| beautiful | hermoso(a) |
| bed | cama |
| beef | carne de res |
| below | debajo |
| best | mejor |
| between | entre |
| bicycle | bicicleta |
| big | grande |
| bike | bici |
| black | negro |
| block (v) | bloquear |
| blond | rubio(a) |
| blue | azul |
| board | pizarrón |
| boil (v) | hervir |
| book | libro |
| bookstore | librería |
| both | ambos |
| box (n) | caja |
| boy | niño |
| brainstorm (v) | hacer lluvia de ideas |
| Brazil | Brasil |
| Brazilian | brasileño(a) |
| bread | pan |
| breakfast | desayuno |
| breaking news | noticias de última hora |
| bring | traer |
| British | británico(a) |
| brother | hermano |
| brown | café (color) |
| build (n) | constitución (física) |
| bully (v) | abusar / hostigar / intimidar |

| English | Spanish |
|---|---|
| bullying (adj) | acosador / intimidatorio |
| bullying (n) | abuso / acoso / intimidación |
| bus | autobús |
| bus stop | parada de autobús |
| but | pero |
| butter | mantequilla |
| buy (v) | comprar |
| café | café / baristería (lugar) |
| cafeteria | cafetería |
| cake | pastel |
| call (v) | llamar |
| Canada | Canadá |
| Canadian | canadiense |
| canyon | cañón |
| car | coche / auto |
| card | tarjeta / carnet |
| Caribbean Sea | Mar Caribe |
| carrot | zanahoria |
| cell phone | teléfono celular |
| central | central |
| cereal | cereal |
| chair | silla |
| chart (n) | gráfica(o) |
| chat (v) | platicar |
| check (v) | corregir / marcar |
| cheese | queso |
| chef | chef |
| chemistry | química |
| chicken | pollo |
| child / children | niño(a) / niños(as) |
| Chile | Chile |
| Chilean | chileno(a) |
| China | China |
| Chinese | chino(a) |
| choose | escoger |
| chop (v) | picar |
| circle (v) | encerrar en un círculo |
| city | ciudad |
| class | clase |
| classmate | compañero(a) de clase |
| classroom | salón de clase |
| closet | closet |
| clothes | ropa |
| clothing | prendas de vestir |

| English | Spanish |
|---|---|
| clue | pista / idea |
| coat | saco |
| coffee | café (bebida) |
| coffee shop | cafetería |
| collect | coleccionar |
| color | color |
| column | columna |
| come from (v) | venir de |
| comment (n) | comentario |
| communication | comunicación |
| community | comunidad |
| complete (adj) | completo(a) |
| complete (v) | completar |
| computer | computadora |
| computer game | juego de computadora |
| consonant | consonante |
| context | contexto |
| conversation | conversación |
| cook (n) | cocinero(a) |
| cook (v) | cocinar |
| cookbook | libro de cocina / recetario |
| cooking (n) | cocción |
| Copper Canyon | Barrancas del Cobre |
| corn | maíz |
| correct (adj) | correcto(a) |
| correct (v) | corregir |
| count noun | sustantivo contable |
| country | país |
| cousin | primo(a) |
| cover (n) | cubierta / portada |
| create | crear |
| crossword puzzle | crucigrama |
| cruel | cruel / malvado(a) |
| culture | cultura |
| cup | taza |
| curly | rizado |
| cyber bully | abusador / acosador cibernético |
| cyber bullying | abuso / acoso cibernético |
| dad | papá |
| daily | diariamente |
| dairy | lácteo |
| date (n) | fecha |
| daughter | hija |

| English | Spanish |
|---|---|
| day | día |
| decide | decidir |
| definition | definición |
| delicious | delicioso(a) |
| describe | describir |
| description | descripción |
| desert | desierto |
| desk | escritorio |
| dictionary | diccionario |
| different | diferente |
| dinner | cena |
| dish | platillo |
| divide (v) | dividir |
| do (v) | hacer |
| doctor | doctor(a) |
| donate | donar |
| download (v) | descargar |
| draw (v) | dibujar |
| drawing (n) | dibujo |
| dream (v) | soñar |
| dress (n) | vestido |
| drive (v) | manejar |
| driver | chofer |
| e-pal | amigo por internet / epal |
| each | cada |
| each other | cada uno |
| early | temprano |
| eat (v) | comer |
| egg | huevo |
| eight | ocho |
| eighteen | dieciocho |
| eighty | ochenta |
| electrical | eléctrico(a) |
| electrician | electricista |
| eleven | once |
| email | correo electrónico |
| embarrassing | penoso(a) |
| embroidery | bordado |
| emergency | emergencia |
| end | final |
| ending | terminación / final |
| England | Inglaterra |
| English | inglés |
| enjoy | disfrutar |
| error | error |
| evaluate | evaluar |
| evaluation | evaluación |
| evening | tarde / noche |

| English | Spanish |
|---|---|
| ever | siempre |
| every | todos(as) / cada |
| evidence | evidencia |
| exchange (n) | intercambio |
| exercise (n) | ejercicio |
| exercise (v) | ejercitar / hacer ejercicio |
| expensive | caro(a) / costoso(a) |
| expression | expresión |
| eye | ojo |
| falls (n) | caída de agua / cascadas |
| false | falso |
| family | familia |
| famous | famoso(a) |
| fast | rápido(a) |
| father | padre |
| favorite | favorito(a) |
| feature | característica |
| feel (v) | sentir |
| feeling | sentimiento |
| fifteen | quince |
| fifty | cincuenta |
| find (v) | encontrar |
| first | primero(a) |
| fish (n) | pez / pescado |
| five | cinco |
| fix (v) | arreglar |
| flight attendant | sobrecargo / aeromoza |
| flour | harina |
| fly (v) | volar |
| folk dance | danza folklórica |
| follow | seguir |
| following (adj) | siguiente |
| fondue | fondú |
| food | alimento / comida |
| for | para |
| form (n) | forma / formulario |
| forty | cuarenta |
| forty-five | cuarenta y cinco |
| four | cuatro |
| fourteen | catorce |
| free time | tiempo libre |
| French | francés |
| frequency | frecuencia |
| fresh | fresco(a) |
| Friday | viernes |
| friend | amigo(a) |

| English | Spanish |
|---|---|
| from | desde /de |
| fruit | fruta |
| fry (v) | freír |
| fun | divertido |
| game | juego |
| gas station | gasolinera |
| geographical | geográfico |
| get to school (v) | llegar a la escuela |
| get up (v) | levantarse |
| give (v) | dar |
| go (v) | ir |
| go shopping (v) | ir de compras |
| go swimming (v) | ir a nadar |
| go to bed (v) | ir a la cama |
| go to school (v) | ir a la escuela |
| good | bueno(a) |
| government | gobierno |
| governor | gobernador(a) |
| grains | granos |
| gram | gramo |
| grammar | gramática |
| grandfather | abuelo |
| grandmother | abuela |
| grandparent | abuelo(a) |
| granola | granola |
| gray | gris |
| great | maravilloso(a) |
| Great Britain | Gran Bretaña |
| green | verde |
| grocery list | lista de compras |
| grocery shopping | ir al supermercado |
| group | grupo |
| guess (v) | adivinar |
| guitar | guitarra |
| guy | chico / tipo |
| gym | gimnasio |
| gymnastics | gimnasia |
| hair | cabello |
| half | medio(a) / mitad |
| half past | y media |
| hamburger | hamburguesa |
| hang out (v) | salir |
| happen (v) | ocurrir |
| hardly ever | rara vez |
| have (v) | tener |
| he | él |
| hear (v) | escuchar |
| height | altura |
| hello | hola |
| help (v) | ayudar |
| her | ella |
| here | aquí |

| English | Spanish |
|---|---|
| hey | eh! |
| hi | hola |
| high school | preparatoria |
| his | suyo / de él |
| home | hogar / casa |
| homework | tarea |
| hot dog | hot dog / perro caliente |
| hotel | hotel |
| house | casa |
| how | cómo |
| how often | con qué frecuencia |
| how old | cuántos años |
| how much / how many | cuánto / cuántos |
| humiliating (adj) | humillante |
| hundred | cien |
| hurt (v) | lastimar |
| hurtful | hiriente |
| I | yo |
| ID | identificación personal |
| ice cream | helado |
| idea | idea |
| ignore | ignorar / no hacer caso |
| imagine | imaginar |
| important | importante |
| in | en / dentro |
| independent | independiente |
| indigenous | indígena |
| information | información |
| ingredient | ingrediente |
| instrument | instrumento |
| interesting | interesante |
| Internet | internet |
| internet café | café internet |
| interview (v) | entrevistar |
| interview (n) | entrevista |
| introduce | presentar |
| introduction | presentación / introducción |
| inventory | inventario |
| investigate | investigar |
| issue | problema / cuestión |
| it | lo |
| Italian | italiano(a) |
| Italy | Italia |
| jacket | chamarra |
| jeans | jeans / pantalones de mezclilla |
| jewelry | joyería / alhajas |
| job | trabajo |
| just | justo(a) |

| English | Spanish |
|---|---|
| justice | justicia |
| karate | karate |
| kilo | kilo |
| know | saber / conocer |
| label (v) | etiquetar |
| lake | lago |
| language | idioma / lengua |
| last name | apellido |
| late | tarde |
| letter | letra |
| life | vida |
| lifestyle | estilo de vida |
| like (v) | gustar |
| like | como |
| line | línea |
| list (n) | lista |
| listen | escuchar |
| listening | escuchando |
| liter | litro |
| live (adj) | en vivo / vivo(a) |
| live (v) | vivir |
| location | ubicación |
| long | largo |
| look at (v) | ver hacia |
| love (v) | amar |
| lunch | almuerzo |
| lyric | letra de canción |
| magical | mágico(a) |
| make (v) | hacer |
| mall | centro comercial |
| many | muchos(as) |
| map | mapa |
| market | mercado |
| match (v) | emparejar / igualar |
| me | mí |
| mean (adj) | grosero(a) |
| measure (v) | medir |
| measurement | medida |
| meat | carne |
| meet (v) | conocer (gente) |
| meeting | junta |
| melt (v) | derretir |
| member | miembro |
| menu | menú |
| message | mensaje |
| Mexican | mexicano(a) |
| Mexico | México |
| midnight | medianoche |
| milk | leche |
| mind map | mapa conceptual |
| mistake (n) | error |
| mix (v) | mezclar |
| mom | mamá |

| English | Spanish |
|---|---|
| moment | momento |
| Monday | lunes |
| more | más |
| morning | mañana |
| mother | madre |
| motorcycle | motocicleta |
| mountain | montaña |
| movie | película |
| movies / movie theatre | cine |
| Ms. | Sra. / Srta. |
| much | mucho(a) |
| music | música |
| musician | músico |
| my | mi |
| myself | yo mismo(a) |
| name | nombre |
| Naples | Nápoles |
| nation | nación |
| nationality | nacionalidad |
| Native American | nativo americano |
| natural | natural |
| need (v) | necesitar |
| negative | negativo |
| never | nunca |
| new | nuevo(a) |
| news | noticias |
| newsstand | puesto de periódicos / revistas |
| next | siguiente |
| next to | al lado de / junto a |
| night | noche |
| nine | nueve |
| nineteen | diecinueve |
| ninety | noventa |
| no | no |
| noncount noun | sustantivo no cuantitativo |
| noon | mediodía |
| not | no |
| nothing | nada |
| notice (v) | notar |
| now | ahora |
| number (n) | número |
| number (v) | numerar |
| nurse | enfermera |
| object | objeto |
| o'clock | en punto |
| ocean | océano |
| of | de |
| often | a menudo |
| OK | Bien. / Está bien. |
| old | viejo |
| on | en / sobre |

| English | Spanish |
|---|---|
| one | uno(a) |
| onion | cebolla |
| online | en línea / conectado |
| or | o |
| orange (adj) | naranja |
| order (v) | ordenar |
| order (n) | orden |
| originally | originalmente |
| other (adj) | otro(a) |
| our | nuestro(a) |
| out | fuera |
| oven | horno |
| over | por encima / a través de |
| overweight | con sobrepeso |
| own | propio(a) |
| Oxford | Oxford |
| Pacific Ocean | Océano Pacífico |
| page | página |
| pants | pantalones |
| paper | papel |
| parent | padre / madre |
| parenthesis | paréntesis |
| park (n) | parque |
| part (n) | parte |
| partner | compañero(a) / pareja |
| passenger | pasajero |
| pasta | pasta |
| patient (n) | paciente |
| peer evaluation | evaluación del compañero |
| pencil | lápiz |
| people | gente |
| per | por |
| perform | actuar |
| person | persona |
| personal | personal |
| Peru | Perú |
| Peruvian | peruano(a) |
| phone | teléfono |
| phrase (n) | frase |
| physical | físico |
| picture | imagen / foto / cuadro |
| pilot | piloto |
| pinch (n) | pizca |
| pink | rosa |
| pizza | pizza |
| place (n) | lugar |
| plan (n) | plan |
| plane | avión |
| play (v) | jugar |

| English | Spanish |
|---|---|
| player | jugador |
| plaza | plaza |
| please | por favor |
| plural | plural |
| point (v) | señalar |
| police officer | oficial de policía |
| poor (adj) | pobre |
| possessive | posesivo |
| post (n) | entrada / texto en un sitio virtual |
| post (v) | postear / subir a internet |
| poster | póster |
| potato | papa |
| pound | libra |
| practice (v) | practicar |
| prefer (v) | preferir |
| preparation | preparación |
| prepare (v) | preparar |
| preposition | preposición |
| present (v) | presentar |
| present continuous | presente contínuo |
| presentation | presentación |
| pretend | fingir / pretender |
| prevent | evitar |
| problem | problema |
| project (n) | proyecto |
| pronoun | pronombre |
| pronunciation | pronunciación |
| protein | proteína |
| protest (n) | protesta |
| protest (v) | protestar |
| purple | morado |
| put (v) | poner |
| puzzle | rompecabezas |
| quantity | cantidad |
| quarter | cuarto |
| question (n) | pregunta |
| questionnaire | cuestionario |
| quiet | silencio |
| radio | radio |
| rainforest | selva |
| rap (n) | rap |
| read (v) | leer |
| reading | leyendo / lectura |
| really | muy / realmente |
| receptionist | recepcionista |
| recipe | receta |
| record (v) | grabar |
| recording | grabación |
| red | rojo |
| Red Cross | Cruz Roja |
| reduced | reducido(a) |

| English | Spanish |
| --- | --- |
| reduction | reducción |
| refrigerator | refrigerador |
| region | región / zona |
| reorder | reordenar |
| repeat (v) | repetir |
| report (n) | informe / reporte |
| report (v) | informar / reportar |
| reporter | reportero(a) |
| represent | representar |
| research (v) | investigar |
| respond | responder |
| response | respuesta |
| responsible | responsable |
| restaurant | restorán / restaurante |
| review (n) | repaso |
| rewrite (v) | reescribir |
| rhythm | ritmo |
| rice | arroz |
| ride (v) | viajar / andar |
| right (correct) | correcto(a) / bien |
| right now | ahora mismo |
| roast (adj) | asado(a) |
| roast (v) | asar |
| role-play (n) | juego de rol |
| role play (v) | jugar roles / interpretar |
| routine | rutina |
| rug | tapete |
| rumor | rumor |
| sad | triste |
| salad | ensalada |
| salt | sal |
| sandwich | emparedado |
| Saturday | sábado |
| sauce | salsa |
| say (v) | decir |
| schedule | horario |
| school | escuela |
| sea | mar |
| see (v) | ver / observar |
| sentence | oración |
| seven | siete |
| seventeen | diecisiete |
| seventy | setenta |
| share (v) | compartir |
| she | ella |
| shirt | camisa |
| shoe | zapato |
| shop (v) | comprar |
| shopkeeper | tendero /vendedor de tienda |
| shopping | compras |

| English | Spanish |
| --- | --- |
| short | corto(a) |
| short | chaparro(a) |
| shorts | pantalón corto |
| shower (n) | regadera |
| simple present | presente simple |
| sing | cantar |
| singer | cantante |
| singular | singular |
| sister | hermana |
| sit | sentarse |
| site | sitio en internet |
| situation | situación |
| six | seis |
| sixteen | dieciseis |
| sixty | sesenta |
| skirt | falda |
| sleep (v) | dormir |
| small | pequeño(a) |
| soccer | fútbol |
| social | social |
| society | sociedad |
| sock | calcetín |
| solution | solución |
| some | algo |
| someone | alguien |
| someone else | alguien más |
| sometimes | algunas veces |
| son | hijo |
| song | canción |
| sorry | perdón / apenado(a) |
| sound (n) | sonido |
| sound (v) | sonar |
| soup | sopa |
| spaghetti | espagueti |
| Spain | España |
| Spanish | español(a) |
| speak | hablar |
| speaking (n) | hablar / hablante |
| spell | deletrear |
| spelling (n) | ortografía |
| spend time (v) | pasar tiempo |
| sport | deporte |
| spread (v) | difundir / esparcir |
| state (n) | estado |
| statement | declaración |
| steak | bistec / filete |
| stick (n) | barra / palo |
| stop (v) | parar / detener |
| story | historia |
| straight | derecho |
| strawberry | fresa |
| street | calle |
| strong | fuerte |

| English | Spanish |
| --- | --- |
| student | estudiante |
| study (v) | estudiar |
| subject (n) | sujeto / materia (de escuela) |
| subway | metro |
| sugar | azúcar |
| Sunday | domingo |
| supermarket | supermercado |
| surf (v) | navegar |
| sweater | suéter |
| sweatshirt | sudadera |
| swimming (n) | natación |
| Switzerland | Suiza |
| tablespoon | cuchara / cucharada |
| taco | taco |
| take (v) | tomar |
| take a shower (v) | tomar un baño / darse una ducha |
| take turns (v) | tomar turnos |
| talk (v) | hablar |
| tall | alto |
| taxi | taxi |
| taxi driver | taxista / chofer de taxi |
| teach | enseñar |
| teacher | professor / maestro |
| team | equipo |
| teaspoon | cuchara de té / cucharita |
| tell (v) | contar / decir |
| ten | diez |
| tennis | tenis |
| test (n) | exámen / prueba |
| text (n) | texto |
| text (v) | textear / mandar un mensaje de texto |
| textiles | textiles |
| thank (v) | agradecer |
| thanks | gracias |
| that | eso |
| the | el |
| their | su / de ellos |
| them | a ellos |
| then | entonces |
| there | ahí |
| these | estos(as) |
| they | ellos(as) |
| thin | delgado(a) |
| thing | cosa |
| think (v) | pensar |
| third | tercero |
| thirteen | trece |
| thirty | treinta |

| English | Spanish |
|---|---|
| this | esto(a) |
| threat | amenaza |
| three | tres |
| Thursday | jueves |
| time | tiempo |
| to | para |
| today | hoy |
| together | juntos(as) |
| tomato | jitomate |
| too | también |
| top | arriba |
| top | blusa sin mangas |
| topic | tema / tópico |
| tortilla | tortilla |
| town | pueblo |
| traditional | tradicional |
| train | tren |
| transportation | transporte |
| tree | árbol |
| true | verdadero |
| T-shirt | camiseta |
| Tuesday | martes |
| turquoise | turquesa |
| TV | televisión |
| twelve | doce |
| twenty | veinte |
| twenty-five | veinticinco |
| two | dos |
| uncle | tío |
| under | abajo |

| English | Spanish |
|---|---|
| underline (v) | subrayar |
| underlined (adj) | subrayado |
| upload (v) | subir a internet |
| use (v) | usar |
| usually | usualmente |
| vegetable | verdura |
| verb | verbo |
| very | muy |
| village | pueblo |
| visa | visa |
| visa application | aplicación de visa |
| visa official | oficial de migración |
| vocabulary | vocabulario |
| vowel | vocal |
| wait for | esperar a |
| waiter | mesero(a) |
| walk (v) | caminar |
| want (v) | querer |
| watch (v) | ver / mirar |
| water | agua |
| waterfall | cascada / caída de agua |
| way | camino / modo |
| we | nosotros(as) |
| wear (v) | usar / vestir |
| weaving (n) | tejido (de telar) |
| Wednesday | miércoles |
| week | semana |
| weekday | entre semana / día de la semana |

| English | Spanish |
|---|---|
| weekend | fin de semana |
| what | qué |
| what time | qué hora |
| when | cuándo |
| where | dónde |
| which | cuál / cuáles |
| white | blanco |
| who | quién / quiénes |
| why | por qué |
| with | con |
| word | palabra |
| wordsearch puzzle | sopa de letras |
| work (n) | trabajo |
| work (v) | trabajar |
| worker | trabajador |
| world | mundo |
| write (v) | escribir |
| writing | redacción / escrito / escritura |
| yeah | sí (informal) |
| year | año |
| yellow | amarillo |
| yes | sí |
| yogurt | yogurt |
| you | tú |
| your | tuyo |
| yourself | tú mismo |
| zero | cero |

## Special phrases

| | | | |
|---|---|---|---|
| Cool! | ¡Genial! | No, thanks. | No, gracias. |
| Do you like …? | ¿Te gusta …? / ¿Le gusta …? | Really? | ¿En serio? / ¿De verdad? |
| Excuse me. | Discúlpeme. / Discúlpame. | That sounds good! | ¡Eso suena bien! |
| Good idea! | ¡Buena idea! | That's cool. | Está padre. |
| Good morning! | ¡Buenos días! | That's OK. | Está bien. |
| Great idea! | ¡Qué gran idea! | What about you? | ¿Qué hay sobre tí? |
| Great! | ¡Maravilloso! | What are you doing? | ¿Qué estás haciendo? |
| Hi! My name's … | Hola, mi nombre es … | What do you do? | ¿A qué te dedicas? |
| How about you? | ¿Qué hay sobre tí? / ¿Qué hay de tí? | What time do you …? | ¿A que hora …? |
| | | What time is it? | ¿Cuál es la hora? |
| How old are you? | ¿Cuántos años tienes? | What's … like? | ¿Cómo es …? |
| I don't know. | No lo sé. | What's the time? | ¿Qué hora es? |
| I think … | Creo que … | What's your name? | ¿Cómo te llamas? |
| I'm sorry. | Lo siento. | Where are you from? | ¿De dónde vienes? |
| Let's … | Vamos a … | Wow! | ¡Órale! |
| Me too! | Yo también. | | |
| Nice. / It's nice to meet you! | Bien. / Mucho gusto. | | |

# Units 1–3 Language summary

## Grammar

### Subject pronouns and possessive adjectives

| Subject pronoun | Possessive adjective | Examples |
|---|---|---|
| I | my | **I** am Brenda. **My** name is Brenda. |
| you | your | **You** are Henry. **Your** name is Henry. |
| he | his | **He** is Juan. **His** name is Juan. |
| she | her | **She** is Sara. **Her** name is Sara. |
| we | our | **We** are Tom and Lily. **Our** names are Tom and Lily. |
| you | your | **You** are Eva and Leo. **Your** names are Eva and Leo. |
| they | their | **They** are Carl and Raul. **Their** names are Carl and Raul. |

- A subject pronoun takes the place of a noun.
- A possessive adjective shows that something belongs to someone.

### Verb *be*

| Affirmative statements | Negative statements |
|---|---|
| You **are** / **You're** in Room B. | You**'re not** in Room C. |
| I **am** / **I'm** Brenda. | **I'm not** Betty. |
| He **is** / **He's** David. | He**'s not** Raul. |
| She **is** / **She's** Sara. | She**'s not** Nancy. |
| It **is** / **It's** in Brazil. | It**'s not** in Spain. |
| We **are** / **We're** in Room B. | We**'re not** in Room C. |
| They **are** / **They're** 15. | They**'re not** 16. |

Contractions:  I'm = I am    you're = you are
he's = he is    she's = she is    it's = it is
we're = we are    they're = they are

| Yes/No questions | Short answers |
|---|---|
| **Am** I in your class? | Yes, you **are**. / No you**'re not**. |
| **Are** you 12 years old? | Yes, I **am**. / No, I**'m not**. |
| **Is** he your father? | Yes, he **is**. / No, he**'s not**. |
| **Is** she in class today? | Yes, she **is**. / No, she**'s not**. |
| **Is** your last name Laredo? | Yes, it **is**. / No, it**'s not**. |
| **Are** you Tom and Lily? | Yes, we **are**. / No, we**'re not**. |
| **Are** they in our class? | Yes, they **are**. / No, they**'re not**. |

## Vocabulary

### Numbers 0–19

0 zero
1 one
2 two
3 three
4 four
5 five
6 six
7 seven
8 eight
9 nine
10 ten
11 eleven
12 twelve
13 thirteen
14 fourteen
15 fifteen
16 sixteen
17 seventeen
18 eighteen
19 nineteen

### Family

aunt
brother
cousin
daughter
father / dad
grandfather
grandmother
mother / mom
parents
sister
son
uncle

### Physical appearance

blue eyes
brown eyes
green eyes
black hair
blond hair
brown hair
gray hair
red hair
curly hair
long hair
no hair / bald
short hair
straight hair
average height
short
tall
overweight
thin

## Question words: Who?, Where?, What?, and How old?

| Questions | Answers |
|---|---|
| **What's** your name? | My name is **Lucy**. |
| **What's** Peru like? | It's **beautiful**. |
| **Who's** Mexican? | **David** is Mexican. |
| **Where** are you from? | I'm from **Brazil**. |
| **How old** is she? | She's **15**. |

Contractions: What's = What is   Who's = Who is

## Possessive 's and s'

| Singular | Plural |
|---|---|
| Leo and Eva are Paolo**'s** cousins. | His cousin**s'** names are Leo and Eva. |

- Possessive 's and s' show that something belongs to someone.

## Verb *have*

| Affirmative statements |
|---|
| I **have** a brother. |
| You **have** two uncles. |
| We **have** six cousins. |
| They **have** brown hair. |
| |
| He **has** blue eyes. |
| She **has** a sister. |
| It **has** beautiful beaches. |

## Articles *a*, *an*, and *the*

| | |
|---|---|
| *a* + consonant sounds | **a** sister <br> **a b**rother |
| *an* + vowel sound | **an a**unt <br> **an** **u**ncle |
| *the* | **the b**each <br> **the** Atlantic ocean <br> **the** Pacific and Atlantic oceans |

- Use *a* and *an* with singular words.
- Use *the* with singular and plural words.

## Countries
Australia
Brazil
Canada
Chile
China
Great Britain
Italy
Mexico
Peru
Spain

## Nationalities
Australian
Brazilian
Canadian
Chilean
Chinese
British
Italian
Mexican
Peruvian
Spanish

## Geographical features
beach
desert
mountain
ocean
rainforest
waterfall

## Common phrases
Hi!
Hello!
It's nice to meet you.
Nice to meet you!
What's your … like?

## Can Do statements
I can introduce myself.

I can talk about and write personal information.

I can talk and write about family members.

I can describe and write about my family, friends, and myself.

I can ask where people are from and describe my favorite natural places.

I can investigate, write, and talk about indigenous cultures.

# Units 4–6 Language summary

## Grammar

### Simple present

| Affirmative statements | | Negative statements | |
|---|---|---|---|
| I | teach. | I | don't teach. |
| You | work. | You | don't work. |
| We | study. | We | don't study. |
| They | have a car. | They | don't have a car. |
| | teaches. | | doesn't teach. |
| He | works. | He | doesn't work. |
| She | studies. | She | doesn't study. |
| | has a car. | | doesn't have a car. |

Contractions: don't = do not   doesn't = does not

- Use the simple present for routines and repeated actions.

### Simple present yes/no questions

| Yes/No questions | | | Short answers |
|---|---|---|---|
| | I | | Yes, you **do**. / No, you **don't**. |
| Do | you | work here? | Yes, I **do**. / No, I **don't**. |
| | we | | Yes, we **do**. / No, we **don't**. |
| | they | | Yes, they **do**. / No, they don't. |
| Does | he | work here? | Yes, he **does**. / No, he **doesn't**. |
| | she | | Yes, she **does**. / No, she **doesn't**. |

### Adverbs of frequency

| Statements | | |
|---|---|---|
| I | always | |
| You | usually | play soccer. |
| We | often | |
| They | sometimes | |
| He | hardly ever | plays soccer. |
| She | never | |

| Questions |
|---|
| Do you **ever** play soccer? |
|   Yes, I do. / No, I don't. |
| Does he **ever** play soccer? |
|   Yes, he does. / No, he doesn't. |

- The adverb usually comes after the subject and before the verb.
- *Sometimes* and *usually* can also go at the beginning of the sentence. *Sometimes, I take the bus to school.*

## Vocabulary

### Jobs
<u>Jobs</u>
chef
musician
nurse
receptionist
student
taxi driver
teacher
waiter
<u>Job activities</u>
answer the phone
bring food
cook food
drive a taxi
help sick people
play an instrument
study
teach

### Transportation
drive a car
ride a bicycle
ride a motorcycle
take a taxi
take the bus
take the train
take the subway
walk

### Activities
go shopping
hang out with friends
listen to music
play computer games
text friends
watch TV

### Sports
do gymnastics
do karate
go swimming
play basketball
play soccer

## Simple present Wh- questions

| Questions | Answers |
|---|---|
| What do you do on Saturdays? | I play basketball. |
| What does she do? | She plays soccer. |
| Where do they play soccer? | At school. |
| Where does he play soccer? | In the park. |
| How do I get to the park? | You walk over there. |
| How does he get to the park? | He takes the bus. |
| Who do we play soccer with? | Our cousins. |
| Who does she play soccer with? | Her friends. |
| When do you play soccer? | On Sundays. |
| When does she play soccer? | On Saturdays. |
| How often do they play soccer? | In the evenings. |
| How often does he play soccer? | Every day. |

## Time expressions

| Phrase | Example |
|---|---|
| on + days of the week | I have classes **on Mondays**. She works **on Thursdays**. |
| on + the weekends / weekdays | We play soccer **on the weekends**. I study **on weekdays**. |
| in + time of day | I check my email **in the mornings**. He goes to class **in the afternoons**. She studies **in the evenings**. |
| every day | We study **every day**. |
| at night | They work **at night**. |

- Use time expressions to say when something happens.

## Prepositions of location

| go + to | other verbs + at / in |
|---|---|
| go **to** the movies | go shopping **at / in** the mall |
| go **to** the mall | check email **at / in** the internet café |
| go **to** the park | exercise **at / in** the gym |
| go **to** the café | play soccer **at / in** the park |
| go **to** school | watch TV **at** home |

- Do not use *the* with *go to school*. We go to school.
  NOT: We go to the school.
- Do not use *in* with *home*. We watch TV at home.
  NOT: We watch TV in home.

## Days of the week
Sunday
Monday
Tuesday
Wednesday
Thursday
Friday
Saturday

## Routines
check email
do homework
eat breakfast
eat dinner
exercise
get up
go to bed
go to school
study
take a shower

## Places around town
gym
internet café
mall
movie theater
movies
park
restaurant

## Common phrases
How about you?
Really?
What about you?

## Can Do statements
I can talk about jobs and work activities.
I can ask and answer questions about transportation.
I can describe and write about free-time activities.
I can talk and write about my daily routine.
I can talk about places around town.
I can investigate, write, and talk about indigenous cultures.

# Units 7–9 Language summary

## Grammar

### Review of simple present Wh- questions

| Questions | Answers |
|---|---|
| **What do** you **do** on Sundays? | **I play** soccer. |
| **What does** she **do** on Saturdays? | She **plays** basketball. |
| **Where do** they **play** soccer? | They play soccer **in the park**. |
| **Where does** he **play** soccer? | He plays soccer **at school**. |
| **Who do** we **play** soccer with? | We play soccer **with our friends**. |
| **Who does** she **play** soccer with? | She plays soccer **with her brother**. |
| **When do** you **play** soccer? | I play soccer on **Saturdays**. |
| **When does** she **play** soccer? | She plays soccer **in the evenings**. |
| **What time** is it? | It's **one fifteen**. |

### Present continuous

| Affirmative statements | Negative statements |
|---|---|
| I'm | I'm |
| You're | You're |
| He's | He's |
| She's  studying. | She's  not studying. |
| We're | We're |
| They're | They're |

- Use the present continuous to show that something is happening now.

### Present continuous yes/no questions

| Yes/No questions | Short answers |
|---|---|
| **Am** I **watching** TV? | Yes, you **are**. / No, you**'re not**. |
| **Are** you **watching** TV? | Yes, I **am**. / No, I**'m not**. |
| **Is** she **watching** TV? | Yes, she **is**. / No, she**'s not**. |
| **Is** he **watching** TV? | Yes, he **is**. / No, he**'s not**. |
| **Are** you and your friends **watching** TV? | Yes, we **are**. / No, we**'re not**. |
| **Are** they **watching** TV? | Yes, they **are**. / No, they**'re not**. |

## Vocabulary

### Telling the time
It's noon. / It's twelve p.m.
It's five o'clock.
It's ten-oh-five. / It's five after ten.
It's a quarter after six. / It's six fifteen.
It's half past four. / It's four thirty.
It's a quarter to two. It's one forty-five.
It's midnight. / It's twelve a.m.

### More jobs
Jobs
accountant
doctor
driver
electrician
flight attendant
pilot
police officer
singer

Job activities
drive a car
fix electrical problems
fly an airplane
help passengers
respond to emergencies
see patients
sing songs
work with numbers

### Colors
black
blue
brown
gray
green
orange
pink
purple
red
white
yellow

### Clothing
dress
jacket
pants
shirt
shoes
skirt
socks
sweater

## Present continuous with Wh- questions

| Questions | Answers |
| --- | --- |
| What **am** I **watching**? | You're watching a movie. |
| What **are** you **watching**? | I'm watching a movie. |
| What **is** she **watching**? | She's watching a movie. |
| What **is** he **watching**? | He's watching a movie. |
| What **are** Eva and Joe **watching**? | They're watching a movie. |
| What **are** you and your friends **watching**? | We're watching a movie. |

## Simple present and present continuous

| Simple present | Present continuous |
| --- | --- |
| I **exercise** every night. | I'**m exercising** now. |
| You **study** on weekdays. | You'**re studying** math now. |
| My dad **works** on the weekends. | He'**s working** now. |
| My friends and I **text** each other. | We'**re texting** each other now. |
| They **walk** to school. | They'**re walking** to school now. |

- Use the simple present for routines.
- Use the present continuous for actions happening now.

### Online activities
chat online
check email
download movies
post a message
read news reports
shop online
surf the Internet
upload pictures

### Cyber bullying
block email and cell phone
collect evidence
ignore (the bully)
make hurtful comments
post embarrassing pictures
pretend to be someone else
report threats
share feelings
spend time doing things you like
spread rumors

### Common phrases
How about this guy?
Look!
Me too!
That's a cool job!
We don't have time for…

### Can Do statements
I can ask for and tell the time.
I can talk about jobs and work activities.
I can talk about activities people are doing right now.
I can describe online activities and daily routines.
I can talk about social issues.
I can write and perform a rap about social issues.

# Units 10–12 Language summary

## Grammar

### There is and there are

| Singular | Plural |
|---|---|
| **There's** a bank here. | **There are** two banks here. |
| **There isn't** a bank here. | **There aren't** two banks here. |

Contractions: there's = there is   isn't = is not   aren't = are not.

- Use there *is/are* to say that something exists.

### Prepositions of location

| Preposition | Example |
|---|---|
| on | There's a bank **on** Oak Street. |
| in | There's a bank **in** the mall. |
| next to | There's a bank **next to** the bus stop. |
| across from | There's a bank **across from** the coffee shop. |
| between | There's a bank **between** the gas station and the hotel. |

- Use a preposition of location to show where something is.

### Count and noncount nouns

| Count nouns and plural spellings | | Noncount nouns |
|---|---|---|
| a carrot | two carrot**s** | beef |
| an apple | two apple**s** | cereal |
| an egg | two egg**s** | cheese |
| a tomato | two tomato**es** | milk |
| a strawberry | two strawberr**ies** | yogurt |

- Count nouns are things you can count. They have plural forms.
- Noncount nouns are things you can't count. They do not have plural forms.

### Is there…? / Are there…?

| Questions | Answers |
|---|---|
| **Is there** any salad? | Yes, **there is**. / No, **there isn't**. |
| **Are there** any hamburgers? | Yes, **there are**. / No, **there aren't**. |

### some, any

| some | any |
|---|---|
| There's **some** ice cream. | There isn't **any** yogurt. |
| There are **some** sandwiches. | There aren't **any** eggs. |

- Use *there's + some* for noncount nouns.
- Use *there are + some* for count nouns.

## Vocabulary

**Places around town**
bank
bookstore
bus stop
coffee shop
gas station
hotel
newsstand
supermarket

**Food**
Dairy
cheese
milk
Fruit
apples
strawberries
Grains
pasta
rice
Vegetables
carrots
potatoes
tomatoes
Meat and protein
beef / steak
chicken
eggs
fish

**On the menu**
hamburger
hot dog
ice cream
pizza
salad
sandwich
soup
spaghetti

## How much...? / How many...?; a lot of, some, a little, a few, much, many, any

| How much + noncount nouns | | |
|---|---|---|
| How **much** soup is there? | | |
| There's | a lot of<br>some<br>a little | soup. |
| There isn't | much<br>any | soup. |

| How many + count nouns | | |
|---|---|---|
| How **many** bananas are there? | | |
| There are | a lot of<br>some<br>a few | bananas. |
| There aren't | many<br>any | bananas. |

### How much is/are...?

| Singular | Plural |
|---|---|
| **How much is** the rice?<br>It's $10 pesos a kilo. | **How much are** the apples?<br>They're $25 pesos a kilo. |

## Measurements and quantities

cup
grams
kilo
liter
pinch
stick
tablespoon
teaspoon

## Cooking verbs

bake
boil
chop
fry
measure
melt
mix
roast

## Numbers 20–101

| Numeral | Word |
|---|---|
| 20 | twenty |
| 30 | thirty |
| 40 | forty |
| 50 | fifty |
| 60 | sixty |
| 70 | seventy |
| 80 | eighty |
| 90 | ninety |
| 100 | a hundred |
| 101 | one hundred and one |

## Common phrases

I don't know.
That sounds good.
I'm really hungry.
Wow!
I'm sorry.
That's OK.
Good idea!
Oh no!
I know how to…
I don't know how to…
Good morning!

## Can Do statements

I can say where places are around town.
I can talk about different foods.
I can talk about food on a menu.
I can talk about measurements and quantities of food.
I can describe different ways to cook food.
I can research recipes and create a cookbook.

# Class audio scripts

## Unit 2
### Exercise 1, Part B [p. 16]
**CD 1, Track 8**

Sergio and Martha are Javier's parents.
Daniel and Javier are their sons.
Ana is their daughter.
Daniel, Javier, and Ana are their children.

1. grandfather
2. grandmother
3. uncle
4. aunt
5. father / dad
6. mother / mom
7. cousin
8. cousin
9. brother
10. sister

## Unit 3
### Exercise 1, Part B [p. 20]
**CD 1, Track 15**

1. beach
2. ocean
3. desert
4. rainforest
5. mountain
6. waterfall

### Exercise 6, Part A [p. 22]
**CD 1, Track 18**

1. Quintana Roo is a state in Mexico. It is on the Caribbean Sea. It has beautiful beaches.
2. The Lancandon rainforest is in the state of Chiapas. It has high mountains. It is famous for the Montebello lakes.
3. Mexico has a big desert in the state of Sonora.
4. The Basaseachic Falls are in the Copper Canyon.

## Unit 4
### Exercise 1, Part A [p. 34]
**CD 1, Track 19**

1. I bring food. I'm a waiter.
2. I answer the phone. I'm a receptionist.
3. I play an instrument. I'm a musician.
4. I help sick people. I'm a nurse.
5. I cook food. I'm a chef.
6. I teach. I'm a teacher.
7. I study. I'm a student.
8. I drive a taxi. I'm a taxi driver.

## Unit 6
### Exercise 1, Part A [p. 42]
**CD 1, Track 32**

1. park
2. mall
3. gym
4. movies, movie theater
5. internet café
6. restaurant

### Exercise 6, Part A [p. 44]
**CD 1, Track 35**

The Triqui basketball team is famous! These basketball players come from Oaxaca. Andres is a Triqui boy. He gets up early every morning. He walks to school. At school, he plays basketball with his friends, of course! Why are the Triqui boys famous? Well, they play basketball with no shoes. The Triqui boys exercise every day. They are strong and fast. Their village has five places to play basketball.

## Unit 7

### Exercise 5, Part A [p. 58]
**CD 2, Track 6**

1. A flight attendant helps passengers.
2. A police officer responds to emergencies.
3. A doctor sees patients.
4. A pilot flies an airplane.
5. An accountant works with numbers.
6. A singer sings songs.
7. An electrician fixes electrical problems.
8. A driver drives a car.

## Unit 9

### Exercise 6, Part A [p. 66]
**CD 2, Track 18**

It's early. No cars on the street. He usually eats breakfast, but not today. He's thinking. He's not listening to music. He is checking his email. He is texting on his phone.

It's late. The house is quiet. She sometimes watches TV, but not tonight. She is playing a computer game. She is reading the news online. She is chatting with friends online. It's late.

## Unit 10

### Exercise 5, Part A [p. 80]
**CD 2, Track 22**

Dairy: cheese, milk
Fruit: apples, strawberries
Grains: rice, pasta
Vegetables: potatoes, tomatoes
Meat and protein: fish, eggs, beef, chicken

## Unit 11

### Exercise 1, Part A [p. 82]
**CD 2, Track 27**

1. ice cream
2. salad
3. pizza
4. soup
5. spaghetti
6. hamburger
7. hot dogs
8. sandwich

### Exercise 5, Part A [p. 84]
**CD 2, Track 30**

1. a tablespoon of milk
2. a teaspoon of sugar
3. a cup of flour
4. a pinch of salt
5. a kilo of fish
6. a hundred grams of cheese
7. half a liter of water
8. a stick of butter

## Unit 12

### Exercise 6, Part A [p. 88]
**CD 2, Track 36**

Good morning! My name is Luigi Giordano. I'm an Italian cook from Naples, Italy. Today, I'm making lunch for friends. It's my favorite recipe. It's called spaghetti al ragú. All my friends love my spaghetti! It's very good! For this recipe, I need salt, tomatoes, onions, cheese and beef. There are fresh vegetables and beef at the market. I always go shopping there. First, I cook a kilo of beef with a pinch of salt. Next, I chop a few tomatoes and some onions. I mix the onions and tomatoes together, then I fry them. I mix the beef with the vegetables and cook them together. Now I boil the spaghetti. Then I put the sauce on the pasta. When the pasta is ready, I melt some cheese on top. Delicious!

# Credits

**Illustrations**

Illustrations by Q2a Media Services.

**Photos**

*Key: L = Left, C = Center, R = Right, T = Top, B = Bottom, B/G = background, (1) or (a) = If image is marked with a number and there are various images.*

1 (a) ©Getty Images/Steve Debenport; 1(b) ©Getty Images/Hero Images; 1 (c) ©Getty Images/Fuse; 1 (d) ©Alamy/David R. Frazier Photolibrary, Inc.; 1 (e) ©Alamy/Anne-Marie Palmer; 1 (f) ©Shutterstock/Hurst Photo; 1 (g) ©Shutterstock/Goodluz; 2 (BR) ©Shutterstock/Peter Kunasz; 6 (a) ©Shutterstock/antoniodiaz; 6 (b) ©Getty Images/Frederic ToutcheCalc; 6 (c) ©Shutterstock/javarman; 6 (d) ©Shutterstock/AlinaMD; 6 (e) ©Shutterstock/LunarVogel; 7 (a) ©Getty Images/Siri Stafford; 7 (b) ©Getty Images/Hongqi Zhang; 7 (c) ©Getty Images/Image Source; 8 (a) ©Getty Images/Jupiterimages; 8 (b) ©Alamy/Lev Dolgachov; 8 (c) ©Getty Images/Hill Street Studios; 8 (d) ©Shutterstock/Andrey Popov; 8 (e) ©Shutterstock/89studio; 8 (f) ©Shutterstock/prapass; 8 (g) ©Alamy/MBI; 8 (h) ©Getty Images/Mark Bowden; 8 (i) ©Getty Images/Steve Debenport; 8 (j) ©Getty Images/londoneye; 8 (k) ©Alamy/Richard G. Bingham II; 8 (l) ©Getty Images/Christopher Futcher; 9 (a) ©Corbis/Rana Faure; 9 (b) ©Getty Images/Image Source; 9 (c) ©Alamy/MBI; 9 (d) ©Getty Images/Mark Bowden; 9 (e) ©Shutterstock/antoniodiaz; 10 (a) ©Shutterstock/bezfamilii; 10 (b) ©Shutterstock/gutval23; 10 (c) ©Shutterstock/Alexlukin; 10 (d) ©Shutterstock/Max Yozhikov; 10 (e) ©Shutterstock/Vasilius; 10 (f) ©Shutterstock/Just2shutter; 10 (g) ©Shutterstock/Edel; 10 (h) ©Getty Images/Ryan McVay; 11 (B/G) ©Alamy/HA Photos; 12 (a) ©Shutterstock/Monkey Business Images; 12 (b) ©Shutterstock/Monkey Business Images; 12 (c) ©Alamy/Lan Shaw; 13 (BR) ©Alamy/PhotoAlto; 14 (BR) ©Alamy/RIA Novosti; 15 (BR) ©Shutterstock/MJTH; 16 (a) ©Shutterstock/Monkey Business Images; 16 (b) ©Shutterstock/Bikeriderlondon; 16 (c) ©Shutterstock/Monkey Business Images; 16 (d) ©Shutterstock/MJTH; 16 (e) ©Shutterstock/Fotoluminate LLC; 16 (f) ©Shutterstock/Wilson Araujo; 16 (g) ©Shutterstock/Jason Stitt; 16 (h) ©Shutterstock/R. Gino SantaMaria; 16 (i) ©Shutterstock/Daniel M Ernst; 16 (j) ©Shutterstock/MJTH; 16 (k) ©Shutterstock/Paul Matthew Photography; 16 (l) ©Shutterstock/Nina Buday; 16 (m) ©Shutterstock/CURAphotography; 18 (a) ©Shutterstock/Iko; 18 (b) ©Shutterstock/Grekov's; 18 (c) ©Shutterstock/Olga Sapegina; 18 (d) ©Shutterstock/Kuleczka; 18 (e) ©Shutterstock/Subbotina Anna; 18 (f) ©Shutterstock/Mettus; 18 (g) ©Shutterstock/Suravid; 18 (h) ©Shutterstock/NinaMalyna; 18 (i) ©Shutterstock/Maria Maarbes; 18 (j) ©Shutterstock/PhilipYb; 18 (k) ©Shutterstock/Aaron Amat; 18 (l) ©Shutterstock/Sergey Nivens; 18 (m) ©Shutterstock/Ilya Andriyanov; 18 (n) ©Getty Images/iStock; 18 (o) ©Alamy/Catchlight Visual Services; 18 (p) ©Shutterstock/Minerva Studio; 20 (a) ©Shutterstock/Lev Kropotov; 20 (b) ©Shutterstock/STILLFX; 20 (c) ©Shutterstock/Mr Doomits; 20 (d) ©Shutterstock/Corund; 20 (e) ©Shutterstock/Jim Barber; 20 (f) ©Shutterstock/Reinhold Leitner; 20 (g) ©Shutterstock/Magicinfoto; 20 (h) ©Shutterstock/The national flag of Mexico; 20 (i) ©Shutterstock/Jim Barber; 20 (j) ©Shutterstock/Marques; 20 (k) ©Shutterstock/Galyna Andrushko; 20 (l) ©Shutterstock/Rabel8; 20 (m) ©Shutterstock/AlexAvich; 20 (n) ©Shutterstock/Justek16; 20 (o) ©Shutterstock/Mariusz Niedzwiedzki; 20 (p) ©Shutterstock/William Berry; 20 (q) ©Alamy/Mark Green; 20 (r) ©Shutterstock; 21 (BR) ©Shutterstock/LDprod; 22 (a) ©Getty Images/Majority World/Contributor; 22 (b) ©Alamy/North Wind Picture Archives; 22 (c) ©Alamy/age fotostock; 22 (d) ©Shutterstock/Newphotoservice; 22 (e) ©Shutterstock/Anton Foltin; 22 (f) ©Shutterstock/Madrugada Verde; 23 (a) ©Alamy/Vladistock; 23 (b) ©Shutterstock/Carolgaranda; 26 (a) ©Shutterstock/Bikerider London; 26 (b) ©Getty Images/Eric Raptosh Photography; 28 (a) ©Shutterstock/Blend Images; 28 (b) ©Shutterstock/Andresr; 28 (c) ©Shutterstock/Blend Images; 28 (d) ©Shutterstock/Monkey Business Images; 28 (e) ©Shutterstock/Monkey Business Images; 28 (f) ©Shutterstock/Serdar Tibet; 28 (g) ©Shutterstock/Felix Mizioznikov; 28 (h) ©Shutterstock/Rob Marmion; 28 (i) ©Shutterstock/Chepe Nicoli; 28 (j) ©Shutterstock/Monkey Business Images; 28 (k) ©Shutterstock/MJTH; 31 (a) ©Alamy/John Mitchell; 31 (b) ©Alamy/Charles O. Cecil; 32 (a) ©Getty Images/Karwai Tang/WireImage; 32 (b) ©Alamy/PhotoAlto; 33 (C) ©Corbis/Moodboard; 34 (a) ©Shutterstock/Dmitry Kalinovsky; 34 (b) ©Shutterstock/Wavebreakmedia; 34 (c) ©Shutterstock/Yakub88; 34 (d) ©Shutterstock/Monkey Business Images; 34 (e) ©Shutterstock/Erwinova; 34 (f) ©Shutterstock/ZouZou; 34 (g) ©Shutterstock/Wavebreakmedia; 34 (h) ©Alamy/David Sanger photography; 34 (i) ©Shutterstock/Mertcan; 34 (j) ©Alamy/Rafael Ben-Ari; 34 (k) ©Shutterstock/Sergey Mironov; 36 (a) ©Alamy/Myrleen Pearson; 36 (b) ©Shutterstock/Luti; 36 (c) ©Shutterstock/Pavel Lysenko; 36 (d) ©Shutterstock/Kekyalyaynen; 36 (e) ©Alamy/David R. Frazier Photolibrary, Inc.; 36 (f) ©Shutterstock/CandyBox Images; 36 (g) ©Alamy/Jeff Greenberg; 36 (h) ©Alamy/Lightworks Media; 36 (i) ©Shutterstock/Monkey Business Images; 38 (a) ©Shutterstock/lithian; 38 (b) ©Shutterstock/Dragon Images; 38 (c) ©Shutterstock/Arek malang; 38 (d) ©Alamy/David R. Frazier Photolibrary, Inc; 38 (e) ©Shutterstock/Wavebreakmedia; 38 (f) ©Shutterstock/Andrey_Popov; 38 (g) ©Shutterstock/Nightman1965; 38 (h) ©Shutterstock/ITALO; 38 (i) ©Shutterstock/Susan Leggett; 38 (j) ©Shutterstock/Monkey Business Images; 38 (k) ©Shutterstock/Monkey Business Images; 38 (l) ©Alamy/RosalreneBetancourt 6; 38 (m) ©Shutterstock/Arek malang; 40 (a) ©Alamy/UpperCut Images; 40 (b) ©Getty Images/Darren Robb; 40 (c) ©Shutterstock/Odua Images; 40 (d) ©Shutterstock/sonya etchison; 40 (e) ©Shutterstock/Martiapunts; 40 (f) ©Alamy/Ted Foxx; 40 (g) ©Alamy/Blend Images; 40 (h) ©Shutterstock/Lisa F. Young; 40 (i) ©Alamy/

Ffotocymru; 40 (j) ©Alamy/Gabriel Baj; 40 (k) ©Getty Images/Amy Eckert; 42 (a) ©Shutterstock/Monkey Business Images; 42 (b) ©Alamy/Danita Delimont; 42 (c) ©Shutterstock/hammett79; 42 (d) ©Alamy/Danita Delimont; 42 (e) ©Alamy/China Photos; 42 (f) ©Alamy/Dbimages; 42 (g) ©Shutterstock/YanLev; 42 (h) ©Shutterstock/Bikeriderlondon; 42 (i) ©Shutterstock/G-stockstudio; 44 (a) ©Corbis/Xinhua Press/Rodrigo Oropeza; 44 (b) ©Shutterstock/Monkey Business Images; 44 (c) ©Getty Images/STF/Miguel Tovar; 44 (d) ©Shutterstock/Aspen Photo; 44 (e) ©Shutterstock/Tumar 45 (a) ©Alamy/Images & Stories; 45 (b) ©Alamy/Keith Dannemiller; 45 (c) ©Alamy/frans lemmens; 45 (d) ©Getty Images/John Elk; 48 (a) ©Alamy/Jeff Greenberg; 48 (b) ©Getty Images/Mark Bowden; 48 (c) ©Corbis/Chris Crisman; 48 (d) ©Alamy/ONOKY/Photononstop; 48 (e) ©Alamy/Image Source; 48 (f) ©Shutterstock/Monkey Business Images; 48 (g) ©Corbis/Marc Romanelli/Blend Images; 48 (h) ©Alamy/David South; 53 (a) ©Alamy/Brian Overcast; 53 (b) ©Shutterstock/Sorin Colac; 55 (B/G) ©Shutterstock/Mandy Godbehear; 56 (a) ©Shutterstock/morenai; 56 (b) ©Shutterstock/NRT; 56 (c) ©Shutterstock/Olga Popova; 56 (d) ©Shutterstock/Patryk Kosmider; 56 (e) ©Shutterstock/ThavornC; 56 (f) ©Shutterstock/Jaroslaw Grudzinski; 56 (g) ©Shutterstock/KKulikov; 56 (h) ©Shutterstock/Jan Petrskovsky; 56 (i) ©Shutterstock/PureSolution; 56 (j) ©Shutterstock/Admin5699; 56 (k) ©Alamy/Juice Images; 56 (l) ©Shutterstock/Monkey Business Images; 56 (m) ©Shutterstock/Milkovasa; 58 (a) ©Shutterstock/Pressmaster; 58 (b) ©Alamy/Migstock; 58 (c) ©Shutterstock/Wavebreakmedia; 58 (d); Shutterstock/Andresr; 58 (e) ©Shutterstock/Photosebia; 58 (f) ©Shutterstock/Pcruciatti; 58 (g) ©Shutterstock/Elnur; 58 (h) ©Shutterstock/Prod-akszyn; 58 (i) ©Alamy/Ace Stock Limited; 59 (BR) ©Shutterstock/Shots Studio; 60 (a) ©Shutterstock/Jeanne McRight; 60 (b) ©Shutterstock/Ruslan Kudrin; 60 (c) ©Shutterstock/Lapina; 60 (d) ©Shutterstock/Jeanette Dietl; 60 (e) ©Shutterstock/BMJ; 60 (f) ©Alamy/PYMCA; 60 (g) ©Shutterstock/Alex Norkin; 60 (h) ©Shutterstock/karkas; 60 (i) ©Shutterstock/Jacek Chabraszewski; 60 (j) ©Shutterstock/Michaeljung; 60 (k) ©Shutterstock/Dragon Images; 62 (a) ©Alamy/Bsipsa; 62 (b) ©Shutterstock/michaeljung; 62 (c) ©Alamy/David J. Green; 62 (d) ©Alamy/Tommy Louth; 62 (e) ©Alamy/Lifestyle themes/David J. Green; 62 (f) ©Alamy/NetPhotos; 62 (g) ©Alamy/Mark Nassal; 62 (h) ©Alamy/LearningStockImages; 62 (i) ©Shutterstock/Goodluz; 64 (a) ©Shutterstock/Christo; 64 (b) ©Shutterstock/Goodluz; 64 (c) ©Shutterstock/Simone van den Berg; 64 (d) ©Alamy/Ace Stock Limited; 66 (a) ©Getty Images/Judith Haeusler; 66 (b) ©Getty Images/Ron Levine; 66 (c) ©Shutterstock/Ariwasabi; 66 (d) ©Alamy/EPF; 67 (a) ©Alamy/Barry Lewis; 67 (b) ©Alamy/Robert Fried; 67 (c) ©Alamy/Benedicte Desrus; 67 (d) ©Getty Images/Clasos/Con; 67 (e) ©Alamy/Pymca; 73 (a) ©Alamy/Chris Rout; 73 (b) ©Getty/Photolibrary; 73 (c) ©Alamy/Bubbles Photolibrary; 73 (d) ©Getty Images/iStockphoto/ispaxiax; 73 (e) ©Alamy/PhotoAlto; 73 (f) ©Alamy/Blend Images; 73 (g) ©Alamy/Pablo Paul; 73 (h) ©Alamy/Art Directors & TRIP; 75 (TR) ©Getty Images/Jack Hollingsworth; 77 (C) ©Getty Images/Image Source; 78 (b) ©Alamy/Barry Lewis; 78 (c) ©Alamy/RosaBetancourt; 78 (d) ©Alamy/John Mitchel; 78 (e) ©Alamy/dbimages; 78 (f) ©1Alamy/dbimages; 78 (g) ©Alamy/greg Ferguson; 78 (h) ©Alamy/Steve Hamblin; 78 (i) ©Alamy/Dorothy Alexander; 78 (j) ©Alamy/CS-Stock; 78 (k) ©Alamy/Agencja Fotograficzna Caro; 78 (l) ©Alamy/Cultura Creative; 80 (a) ©Shutterstock/aarrows; 80 (b) ©Shutterstock/Hurst Photo; 80 (c) ©Shutterstock/Valery121283; 80 (d) ©Shutterstock/Gerasimova Inga; 80 (e) ©Shutterstock/Elena Elisseeva; 80 (f) ©Shutterstock/Elena Schweitzer; 80 (g) ©Shutterstock/Wiktory; 80 (h) ©Shutterstock/Valentyn Volkov; 80 (i) ©Shutterstock/Yevgen Sundikov; 80 (j) ©Shutterstock/JIANG HONGYAN; 80 (k) ©Shutterstock/Kondor83; 80 (l) ©Shutterstock/Jane Rix; 80 (m-1) ©Alamy/ACE STOCK LIMITED; 80 (m-2) ©Shutterstock/George Dolgikh; 82 (a) ©Shutterstock/Anna©Pustynnikova; 82 (b) ©Shutterstock/B.and E. Dudzinscy; 82 (c) ©Shutterstock/Jacek Chabraszewski; 82 (d) ©Shutterstock/Kjetil Kolbjornsrud; 82 (e) ©Shutterstock/Olga Nayashkova; 82 (f) ©Shutterstock/Shaiith; 82 (g) ©Shutterstock/Brent Hofacker; 82 (h) ©Shutterstock/Brent Hofacker; 82 (i) ©Alamy/Geraint Lewis; 84 (a) ©Shutterstock/marekuliasz; 84 (b) ©Alamy/Niall McDiarmid; 84 (c) ©Getty Images/Harri Tahvanainen; 84 (d) ©Shutterstock/Daniel Taeger; 84 (e) ©Alamy/Crystite; 84 (f) ©Alamy/Image Source; 84 (g) ©Alamy/foodfolio; 84 (h) ©Shutterstock/Stargazer; 84 (i) ©Shutterstock/Arina P Habich; 86 (a) ©Shutterstock/auremar; 86 (b) ©Alamy/Zoonar GmbH; 86 (c) ©Shutterstock/silentwings; 86 (d) ©Shutterstock/Darryl Brooks; 86 (e) ©Alamy/BlueMoon Stock; 86 (f) ©Shutterstock/Sergey Chayko; 86 (g) ©Alamy/foodfolio; 86 (h) ©Alamy/Leigh Anne Meeks; 86 (i) ©Shutterstock/cdrin; 87 (a) ©Alamy/David Young-Wolff; 87 (b) ©Alamy/Image Source Salsa; 87 (c) ©Shutterstock/Aleph Studio; 88 (a) ©Shutterstock/LogicheCreative.it; 88 (b) ©Shutterstock/marco mayer; 89 (a) ©Shutterstock/Shandor; 89 (b) ©Shutterstock/Ildi Papp; 89 (c) ©Shutterstock/bonchan; 89 (d) ©Alamy/Robert Harding Picture Library Ltd; 89 (e) ©Alamy/Ashok Saxena; 97 (TR) ©Getty Images/Altrendo images.

# Notes

# Notes

# Notes

# Notes

# Notes